Aggression in Our Children

Aggression in Our Children

Henri Parens, M.D.

In collaboration with

Elizabeth Scattergood, M.A.
William Singletary, M.D.
Andrina Duff, M.S.S.

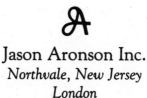

Jason Aronson Inc.
Northvale, New Jersey
London

The author gratefully acknowledges the following people for permission to include photographs in this book:

Erika Stone, photographer, for furnishing the photographs on pages 34, 63, 98, and the cover.

The following mothers for providing pictures of their children: Denise Rowe, Harriet Sumsky, Leslie Goldsmith, Lynn Reiheld-Erney, and Donna M. Hewins.

Library of Congress Cataloging-in-Publication Data

Parens, Henri, 1928–
  Aggression in our children.

  Includes index.
  1. Aggressiveness in children. 2. Child rearing.
3. Parent and child. I. Title [DNLM: 1. Aggression—in infancy & childhood. 2. Child Rearing. 3. Parent–Child Relations. WS 350.8.A4 P228a]
BF723.A35P37 1987   155.4'18   87-19547
ISBN 0-87668-979-9

Manufactured in the United States of America.

TO THE MOTHERS
AND THEIR CHILDREN—
WHO HELPED US LEARN
MUCH OF WHAT WE KNOW

Contents

Preface

Our experience working with parents and children has convinced us that handling children's aggression is one of the most difficult challenges for parents. In turn, children often encounter significant problems in dealing with their own aggression, and as adults many will continue to have difficulty. The constructive management of aggression greatly contributes to both the proper future emotional development of the child and the comfort of the parents.

In this book we talk to parents, mental health professionals who work with parents and children, pediatricians, teachers, and other child caregivers. In the course of our research on aggression in young children, we have found a number of parent–child interactions in which aggression is especially activated. In these, aggression is generated or mobilized especially in the form of anger, hostility, hate, and rage – what we speak of as hostile destructiveness. Our research and our clinical work has shown that parental input and handling significantly influence the development of aggression, in both its nondestructive form – assertiveness—and in its destructive form—hostility. The challenge for the parent is to promote what is healthy in aggression, that which is needed for adaptation, and to mitigate what is hostile, that which can interfere with children's well-being. We are convinced that informing parents about inherent features and dynamics of aggression and proposing strategies for their parenting interventions can help them in this challenge.

We first present the reader with our model of aggression, which developed out of our learning to understand what aggression is and what causes it. This model provides us with the means for exploring, understanding, and developing strategies to deal constructively with a cluster of frequently occurring parent–child interactions in which the two basic forms of aggression—assertiveness and hostility—are at play. If we can help parents attain a clearer understanding of typical aggression interactions between them and their children, they will be able to apply this basic knowledge to other parent–child interactions.

The issues we address are complex, and some may not be easily assimilated at first reading. There are, however, no unexpected rocks, whirlpools, or dragons. Our aim is to help parents seize the rich opportunities inherent in these challenging interactions with their children.

Acknowledgments

We want to thank the many parents and their children who participated in the various parent–infant groups we have worked with since 1970, at both the Eastern Pennsylvania Psychiatric Institute (The Medical College of Pennsylvania) and the Germantown Friends School. What we learned by observing and working with them complemented our body of clinical work and research.

We are also indebted to a number of collaborators who over the years have made our work possible. We especially would like to express personal gratitude to Peter G. Bennett, M.D., Elaine Frank, M.S.W., Estelle Harris, R.N., Rogelio C. Hernit, M.D., Betty Ives-Adams, M.Ed., Leafy Pollock, Ph.D., and Denise Rowe.

Our appreciation is owed to those in the Department of Psychiatry at The Medical College of Pennsylvania who have supported our work for nearly two decades, from the past chairman of the department, Leo Madow, M.D., the past chief of child psychiatry at the Eastern Pennsylvania Psychiatric Institute, Robert C. Prall, M.D., to the present chairman of the department, Wagner Bridger, M.D., the current director of training in child psychiatry, Joel B. Goldstein, M.D., and the vice chairman and director of child psychiatry, Susan V. McLeer, M.D. We feel special gratitude to Selma Kramer, M.D., past chief of the division of child psychiatry at The Medical College of Pennsylvania, as a mentor, a collaborator, and a strong supporter of our work.

We also want to thank Lorraine Slepian, R.C.S.W., and Michael Stept, M.D., for reading our manuscript and making suggestions to improve it. We also owe a special debt to Patsy Turrini, R.C.S.W., and Lorraine Slepian, R.C.S.W., from The Mothers' Center (Hempstead, New York), at whose urgings we undertook to write this book.

Special thanks to Leora Kahn for her help with the photographs that richly illustrate our thoughts. Finally, a very special thanks to Mrs. Harriet Sumsky for her numerous typings of the manuscript, her suggestions, and her steadfast support in this effort.

Aggression in Our Children

CHAPTER 1

Why Do We Need to Understand Aggression?

There would be no point helping parents understand what aggression is, where it comes from, or what causes it, were it not for the fact that dealing with our children's hostility—toward us, others, and themselves—is among the most troublesome tasks of parenting. Difficult and unpleasant as it is for us to admit, it is unavoidable that our children—little ones, grade-school ones, and adolescents—will at times hate us, wish they could be rid of us, and then dread the thought ever after. Often we seem pressured from within to deny this.

A 30-month-old, upset because Mother reasonably prohibits his taking a toy from another child, half shouts at her, "I hate you!" Troubled, the mother—who knows that children are less able than adults to control the expression of their feelings—tells him, "I know you don't mean that." Unfortunately, this is not a helpful comeback. Why it is not helpful is what we will talk about.

It is equally unavoidable that we, as parents, will at times be furious with our children and, because we love them, feel terrible about it afterward. Few experiences produce more guilt and shame in good parents than those moments when we feel, "I would like to be rid of that little. . . ."

Ambivalence—being angry with and even hating a person we love—is experienced in all primary relationships. These are the relationships most meaningful to us: between parents and children, between siblings, between boyfriend and girlfriend, between husband and wife. Being angry with or hating those we love is a large source of difficulty in our close relationships.

The endowment with which we are born—which makes some of us more vulnerable to emotional pain and irritability than others—plus the experiences we have in the course of our growing up, contribute centrally to the kind of individual, friend, mate, and parent we become. In turn, the best we as parents can do is help our children learn to cope well with the hardships of growing up and become individuals who can enjoy loving and being loved, working and being creative, relaxing and having fun. All of these are going to be influenced by the way our children learn to cope with their aggression.

Our aggression—in its forms both of assertiveness (nondestructive aggression) and of hostility and hate (hostile destructiveness)—influences our emotional development, the formation of our personality, the state of our emotional well-being, and our mental health. We cannot emphasize too strongly that helping our children learn to handle their aggression constructively has large implications for their well-being and development as individuals and social beings.

Understanding Your Child's Behavior Helps
You Devise Strategies for Child Rearing

When we understand a problem, we are more likely to know how to solve it. When we understand what our child's behavior is about, we can parent more reasonably, more constructively, and with more confidence; our child-rearing strategies are more likely to work. There is much that parents understand, and much they do well, without recourse to the help of others or books. Much of what we do that is based on what we feel, understand, and believe will, indeed, be best for our children. However, at times even the best of parents find themselves in a quandary about what to do, particularly with respect to aggressive behavior.

We have had the privilege and opportunity to study and work—clinically and educationally[1]—for over two dec-

---

[1]Since 1970, our work with parents and their young children has formally turned to education for parenting. We have developed two methods for this work. First, we use a group method for teaching parenting to people who are already parents. A group consists of seven to ten mothers (and fathers, where feasible) with all their preschool children, who meet for a one-and-a-half-hour weekly session with two mental health professionals knowledgeable in child development. Members continue in the group, which is open-ended, for as long as they wish. In a natural setting, we talk about the behaviors occurring in the children that are puzzling or troublesome to the parents. We also discuss any questions the parents have about their children or their parenting. Groups of this kind have met for several years, in the course of which we have seen mothers of all educational levels acquire much understanding of their children's emotional experiencing and the

ades—with parents and their children. From this work and from our personal experiences as parents, we have gained much respect for parents, for their devotion, ingenuity, and all-consuming efforts to rear their children well. We have learned well what a taxing and challenging job parenting is!

Also, we have learned that there is much information available to mental health professionals that can be of great use to all of us in our work of parenting. To a degree never available to us before, mental health clinicians and researchers have enlarged our understanding of children's behavior and what they require for healthy development. The study of infants and children over the past half century has given us information that, if made available to parents, can inform and help them in their parenting work. Here, we will focus on children's aggression, which we are convinced is a central matter. Once parents understand several key interactions that are emotionally significant to their children and challenging to their parenting, then, with parental ingenuity, they can apply what they have learned about dealing with aggression to other areas of child–parent interaction.

---

psychodynamics of their behaviors, and from that develop a basis for more growth-promoting child rearing.

The second method is to teach parenting to students—parents-to-be—from kindergarten through grade 12. We continue to develop a curriculum encompassing the emotional sector of parenting (Parens et al., work in progress). Preliminary field applications of this method by us and that of an introductory curriculum devised by Heath and colleagues (1986) show promising results and much student interest.

CHAPTER 2

What Is Aggression and What Causes It?

Let's establish what we mean by *aggression*. Aggression is not uniformly defined. One reason for this is that different behaviors are subsumed under the heading of aggression. For example, hostility is a form of aggression we know to be very troublesome, both to ourselves and others. Assertiveness, on the other hand, is a form of aggression that can serve us well in achieving our goals; indeed, we cannot do without it. Also, we do not all mean the same thing when we call some behavior aggressive. Some scientists, for instance, do not speak of assertiveness as aggression. Like many others, we do.

Several available models could serve us nicely in talking about handling our children's aggression. Here is one that we developed out of our work. It has served us well.

A Working Model for Understanding Aggression

Our own naturalistic studies of normal young children and their parents (mothers, for the most part) have shown us that aggression manifests itself in different forms that are evident in even very young children. All of these forms (and behaviors) of aggression have one common feature: They are an attempt to control, act upon, and master ourselves and our environment, including the people within it. These aggressive behaviors seem to be propelled by inborn mechanisms, or by an inner "force," that motivate them.

Let us emphasize that ours is not a model of aggression developed in an isolated armchair. Quite the contrary. We were pushed to study aggression when we found that young children's behaviors put into question some of our past theorizing about aggression. To resolve this problem, we set out to look afresh at children's aggressive behaviors. Early in the course of our observations of young children and their parents, we were faced with a confusing, bewildering array of behaviors, all of which we classified as aggressive. However, we found that certain types of aggressive behaviors seem vastly different from others. For example: An infant's exploratory behaviors, or a child's pressured efforts to make something happen, differ significantly from a hungry infant's rageful crying or a young child's teasing and taunting another. With much effort, we were able to distinguish several categories of aggressive behavior.[1]

For the sake of clarity and emphasis, we will confine our

---

[1]For a more complete explication of our model of aggression, the reader is referred to H. Parens, *The Development of Aggression in Early Childhood* (New York: Jason Aronson, 1979).

discussion of aggression to the two major forms that confront us as parents. The first is *nondestructive aggression*, which we see in assertive, nonhostile, self-protective, goal-achieving, and mastery behaviors. The evidence suggests that nondestructive aggression is the product of an inborn system that serves adaptation and the attaining of our wishes and goals. This system is present and functioning, however primitively, at birth.

The second is *hostile destructiveness*, which we see in angry, nasty, hurtful behaviors: hate, rage, bullying, torturing, vengefulness, and the like. Although hostile destructiveness is self-protective, it causes many individual and collective problems and suffering for humans. In contrast to nondestructive aggression, hostile destructiveness is *not* present at birth. What is present at birth is the mechanism for its production (generation) or mobilization. What activates the mechanism and generates hostile destructiveness, even in its most primitive form in infancy, is *the experience of excessive unpleasure (excessive pain or distress)*.

These are the forms of aggression that concern us most in child rearing. Our entire emotional life is influenced by them. Both of these forms of aggression are shaped by the experiences our children have, especially the experiences we provide as parents. Let's talk a bit more about each of these major forms of aggression.

First, there is a form of aggression that is inherently not destructive and inherently not hostile. We find evidence of such nondestructive aggression in the behavior of children as early as the first months of life. We believe the aim of this nondestructive aggression is to assert oneself upon, control, and thrust oneself toward mastery of one's self and one's environment. This type of aggression is a large motivational force inherent in efforts to develop and become competent and self-reliant. It also motivates self-fulfilling competitiveness that is not primarily hostile and destructive. It serves to secure and protect our needs, property, and rights. It propels and sustains our self-determination and is intimately tied up with the achievement of our personal wishes and aims, as well as our capacities to adapt. Indeed, a sufficient capacity to experience this type of aggression is essential for healthy adaptation.

This type of aggression can be inferred from an infant's exploratory behaviors or a child's or teenager's pressured

Nondestructive aggression is fueling this child's drive up a tree. This is essential for healthy emotional development.

efforts to make something happen. This is especially clear in an infant's exploratory behavior that appears pressured, where we see the infant's determination to get hold of what is drawing his or her interest.

> For example, during feeding, 3¹/₂-month-old Jane's hand reaches for the spoon Mother is bringing to Jane's mouth. She latches onto it quite firmly, and appears to participate in the feeding process. Later the same morning, she explores a set of plastic rings on a string. She stares at them, grabs hold of them, stretches them, mouths them, stares at them some more, mouths them again—over and over— with much pressure and persistence, giving the impression that she is fascinated by this new (to her) thing and needs to learn what it is.

Here we see Jane's effort to be on top of something new—an inner pressure to control something in her environment, to make it do what she wants it to do. This is done with no anger or annoyance, and with no intention of destroying or bringing harm to it. We begin to see this type of activity in infants from the first months of life. It occurs during periods of alert wakefulness—when the infant is emotionally and physically comfortable and gives the impression of being attracted to the environment and wanting to explore it.

Next let's look at the form of aggression designated *hostile destructiveness*. This includes angry and hostile behaviors associated with experiences of intense distress and pain, as well as hostile, destructive behavior that is expressed with pleasure and the overt wish to hurt.

We have seen much behavior in children that has aggressive features identifiable as hostility. In fact, we have seen the earliest forms of such behaviors from the first days of life. Rage reactions are even possible in newborns. We believe these rage reactions to be the most primitive form of hostility in humans. Of course, in the first months of life, the infant having a rage reaction does not think about wanting to destroy anything or anyone. To the best of our knowledge, in the first months of life infants are not able to have such thoughts or experience that intention. The ability to experience such wishes does not arise, we assume, until about the middle of the first year of life. From near the end of the first year of life on, rage reactions in children clearly give the impression that the child experiences hostility and often with it, the wish to cause harm. For example, such a feeling can be inferred from the angry flinging of a toy when a child is unwillingly placed in his crib.

Looking at infants (even before they are capable of thoughts and wishes to destroy) has led us to propose that there is always a trigger for a rage reaction. Indeed, this is true for all acts of hostility. That trigger is the experience of excessive pain or distress. We have spoken of it as *excessive unpleasure.* We have found, over years of observing young children, that (as all parents know intuitively) whenever a child experiences a rage reaction, something is causing it.

It is only when parents have tried all they know to do, are at their wits' ends, and cannot identify the source of excessive pain or distress, that they resort to the explanation that children need to cry "to exercise their lungs." We believe this to be a false explanation for children's crying. One good thing about children's crying is that they are

Failure to get his big sister out of *his* sandbox is upsetting David.

letting themselves express the pain (of whatever sort) they are feeling. That is generally desirable. But our point here is that whenever an infant experiences rage, it is because he has experienced excessive pain or distress in one form or another—some type of excessive unpleasure. This condition is a prerequisite for the experience of rage.[2]

From this and related behaviors, we have come to believe that all *feelings of hostility owe their existence to an underlying experience of excessive pain or emotional distress.* The excessive distress changes the inherently nondestructive aggressive tendency to assert oneself and control one's environment

---

[2]In rare instances in childhood, some children with brain disorders— such as those that cause epileptic seizures—may have rage reactions that may not be triggered by experiences of excessive unpleasure. These we assume to be uncommon.

His efforts to get her out are fueled by aggression (assertiveness). As unpleasure mounts, though, *hostility* will be generated. [Were this to go on, hostility would mount and David would (1) lash out at his sister, or (2) give up and the hostility would stay within him, or (3) reason that he had better turn his interest elsewhere and defend against the hostility already generated by this experience, or (4) some combination of these.]

into wanting (needing) to cause harm to whatever is believed to be the source of the excessive pain or distress. This type of aggression then has the feature of being pressured from within to cause harm to or to eliminate from one's environment what is perceived to be causing the excessive unpleasure.

At a very early age, children's efforts to manage feelings of hostility lead them to use ways of coping that will make their hostility and rage tolerable and its discharge and enactment feasible. For example, we have seen a 14-month-old girl who was angry with her mother. She began to throw a wooden block at her mother, but instead, she slightly rotated her body and threw the block at the leg of a woman who was sitting *next* to her mother. She had displaced the hostile feelings she was experiencing toward her mother, and the hostile act to which it led, from the mother she loved to somebody else—who it seemed less threatening to attack. As she did so, she smiled smugly.

In another instance, we saw 14-month-old Candy walk up to 2¹/₂-year-old Donny and strike him one solid blow on the arm. We were not surprised at her doing so, as three days before, Donny had struck Candy harshly. At the time she had cried, but we had seen no act of aggression directed against Donny. Instead, Candy displaced her hostile feelings onto her sister Cindy and onto toys. Now, three days later, Candy seemed to calculatedly lash out, to unleash her hostile feelings toward Donny. Young as she was, she appeared calm, in control of herself, and prepared for this action. She did not look as though she was thoroughly enjoying what she was doing, but there was an air of defiance and self-satisfaction about her.

Now let's turn to another example, this time to hostile behavior that is expressed with pleasure and the overt wish to be hurtful. This kind of behavior becomes evident in children from about 1 year of age, in behavior that we can identify as teasing and taunting.

Two-and-a-half-year-old Susan seemed rather restless one morning. As she went from one toy to another, she noted with interest a toy $1^1/_2$-year-old Tommy was exploring. With a half smile on her face, she reached for that toy and pulled it from Tommy's hand. Her mother was looking elsewhere and did not see this. Within moments, Susan—again smiling—grabbed the next toy Tommy picked up. Again, she watched Tommy's reaction with some satisfaction. Tommy fussed. He picked up yet another toy, and in a moment, Susan grabbed it. Her smile now conveyed a feeling of pleasure at being nasty to Tommy. Now Tommy was heard, and Susan's mother tuned in to what was going on.

We inferred that these children were acting on feelings of hostility that had been mobilized within them by events that occurred before the hostile act was carried out. With Candy, we had seen the attack on her three days before by the youngster who became her target. We concluded that hostile acts in children—those that are carried out under conditions of pleasure and/or premeditation—are preceded by an experience of excessive pain that has been recorded in the psyche. This hostility is acted on later, under conditions that are easier for the child to deal with. In other words, when children or adults act sadistically to harm another person, we assume they do so because they have previously suffered significant injury to their emotional self. Injury to our narcissism (our sense of self-love and self-regard) is a major source of such acts.

Thus, hostile destructiveness—like the other types of aggression—is basically an act of asserting oneself over and controlling oneself and one's environment. Under the influence of excessive distress or pain, it becomes a wish to inflict pain and effect the destruction of the thing or person being controlled. We believe this is what hostility, hate, and rage are about.

This form of aggression is what makes for ambivalence in human relationships. This is the form of aggression that mental-health clinicians know can create enormous emotional conflicts, lead to excessive guilt and the development of harsh consciences, create havoc in our capacities to adapt and develop good relationships, and much more.

Implications for Parenting

The implications of this model of aggression for parenting are large. First of all, we cannot deal with all aggressive behaviors in the same way. In fact, it is highly undesirable to do so. To help our children learn to adapt to our world, it has to be possible for them to be aggressive at certain times in certain ways and not be aggressive at other times in other ways. "What should I do if my child hits another child?" is a question we have often heard. To know what to do, one has to know the characteristics of the given child, the context in which the child is hitting another child, and the history of the child's relationship to the other. Is he attacking the other child? Is he defending his own possession? Is he retaliating for a prior attack by the other child? In other words, is he being self-protective, or is he being hostile, displacing rage from elsewhere onto an innocent bystander?

Aggression, we emphasize, is not one thing. On the one

hand, it may be inherently nonhostile and serve adaptation, the protection of oneself and one's rights, the fulfillment of one's wishes and aims. Appropriately expressed, aggression plays an important part in our capacity to adapt, to learn, as well as to succeed in our enterprises.

On the other hand, aggression can take the form of hostility and hate. It can lead to the wish—even to the need—to hurt others, and to the need to hurt oneself. It can lead to the production of bullies and to the production of children terrified to stand up for themselves. Both are products of hostile aggression. It can lead to pain and to the destruction of our own aims and wishes, as well as to the destruction of the environment. In extreme forms, it can lead to the destruction of those around us, even those we love and ourselves.

The first type of aggression is highly desirable and necessary for achievement and survival. The second type leads to hurt and pain, even though it may be necessary for adaptation and survival at times. Looking at it from the vantage point of the parent with regard to his or her own child, we want to help our children learn to become healthily assertive in its nondestructive form: to be able to assert themselves where desirable, to sustain their efforts in mastering a task, and to mobilize their energies toward achieving their aims and goals. On the other hand, we do not want our children to be hostile to themselves or unnecessarily hostile to others, nor do we want them to do things that are damaging to themselves or society. We do not want them to be riddled with internal conflicts, guilt, and shame. We want our children to respect themselves, to respect others, and to be socially responsible, as well as able to form good love relationships, work effectively, and enjoy their lives sufficiently.

Having an appreciation of the fact that aggression can be nondestructive and fuel autonomy and assertiveness, and that it can be hostile and destructive can make clearer the answer to the question, "What should I do if my child hits another child?"

The degree of hostility generated in the child influences the quality of the child's well-being. We all recognize the havoc that excessive hostility produces in our world: crimes in the home and on the street, preparations for and the carrying out of wars, and the unprecedented and highly threatening nuclear arms race. Although as parents we are highly concerned about these issues, it is not our intention here to address issues at that level of social concern, but simply to underline that unresolved problems of hostile destructiveness can have widespread consequences.

Here we want to talk about the implications of hostility for the well-being of our individual children. To inflict pain or harm and to destroy that which causes us pain and distress, is quite understandable. This is what hostility, hate, and rage are all about. Difficult as it is to accept, we have to recognize that some degree of hostility is unavoidable in our children. Even in the best of worlds and families, normal disappointments and restrictions on the gratification of wishes are often needed to rear a child in a growth-promoting way. In other words, good parents will unavoidably elicit hostility in their children, even in the course of loving and growth-promoting rearing. Modest levels of hostility may create modest degrees of difficulty within the child. This cannot be avoided. However, to a substantial degree, we can modulate both the frequency and intensity of hostility generation and mobilization. Therefore, we can protect our children against experiencing *excessive* levels of hostility. In this way, we can be of particular help to them.

Fortunately, in most instances with most children, we are capable of preventing the development of excessive hostility. Since hostility is mobilized by experiences of excessive pain and/or distress, if we can find ways to prevent or lessen the impact of their experiencing excessive unpleasure, we will prevent or lessen the generation of hostility in them. There is a way of preventing the generation of excessive hostility in our children while recognizing that hostility in moderate degrees cannot and does not need to be prevented. A number of years ago,[3] we made several recommendations to those concerned with children.

We can help parents, caregivers, teachers, and other child tenders learn and recognize that excessive unpleasure experiences generate or mobilize hostility in the child. The key phrase is *excessive unpleasure*. The caution is twofold: First, experiences of unpleasure are unavoidable; second, benign experiences of unpleasure lead to adaptation, learning, and growth. Benign experiences of unpleasure lead to efforts to master and improve our life situation. For instance, even infants have built-in adaptive mechanisms

---

[3]H. Parens, *The Development of Aggression in Early Childhood* (New York: Jason Aronson, 1979).

that become activated when they experience discomfort. Infants adapt to benign levels of unpleasure by putting their thumbs or pacifiers in their mouths. In doing so they are adapting, they are learning to soothe themselves. In fact, they are learning to be independent. It is when unpleasure is felt as excessive that it may wreak havoc in the individual.

Children ought to be protected against too frequent and too prolonged excessive unpleasure experiences. It is important for parents and other child tenders to know that children vary widely in the way they tolerate unpleasure. We all have different thresholds of irritability and pain tolerance. During the child's earliest years, parents should study their child's ways of expressing the experience of excessive unpleasure. Each child has his or her own unique combination of behavioral and vocal ways of expressing feelings of excessive unpleasure. We are calling for parents to further develop their innate ability to feel what their child is experiencing and to look for those expressions that signal the experience of excessive unpleasure.

Parents need to know that there are ways of enhancing a child's capability to modify the hostility generated within the child. This capability, in large part, depends on the child's having a good relationship with his or her parents. Each child has the capability to lessen the amount and mitigate the intensity of hostility that life circumstances generate within him or her. A sufficiently positive attachment to his/her mother or father is necessary for the development of that potential capability. A loving, generally positive emotional relationship will help the child cope better with his or her hostility. Thus, the child can be spared a great deal of pain and can better secure for himself or herself a greater degree of well-being. A good emotional relationship with our children has far-reaching implications, not only in the area of aggression, but in all dimensions of emotional life.

We are convinced, from our work with parents and children, that parents can be helped to intervene constructively in their children's lives and lessen the production and mobilization of hostility, as well as help them cope in growth-promoting ways with the unavoidable experiences of excessive unpleasure and hostility. In the course of our studies in aggression and in education for parenting, we have identified specific areas of parent–child interaction and experience where hostility most commonly becomes generated or mobilized. These are also the areas of interaction where nondestructive aggression can be protected and enhanced.

These are:

1. Dealing constructively with the child's experiencing excessive unpleasure.
2. Recognizing the need for—and allowing children—sufficient and reasonable autonomy and exploratory/learning/practicing activity.
3. Setting limits constructively.
4. Teaching the child how to express and discharge anger and hostility in reasonable and acceptable ways.
5. Handling the child's rage reactions and temper tantrums in growth-promoting ways.

6. Helping the child cope with painful emotional feelings such as anxiety and depression.
7. Optimizing the parent–child relationship.

In following chapters we will discuss dealing with aggression in each of these areas of parent–child interaction. We will do so from the vantage point of providing a rationale for parenting intervention, and we will propose general steps that can be taken to achieve growth-promoting parenting. We will not address all aspects of aggressive behavior in children; this is neither feasible nor necessary. In the process of exploring these seven types of parent–child interactions, parents will learn much that can also be applied in other circumstances.

Our prime aim is to help parents gain a better understanding of their children's behavior and aggression. Based on such understanding, they will be able to develop helpful strategies for intervening with their children. We feel that if parents do this, they will be able to deal more constructively with the hostility that life experiences often unavoidably mobilize in the child and in themselves.

CHAPTER 3

Dealing Constructively with Excessive Unpleasure Experiences

Three-month-old Kathy has been making fussing sounds for a minute. She quiets. Thirty seconds later, she begins to fuss again, this time a bit more loudly. Again, she quiets. About 20 seconds later, her fussing starts again, intensifies, and now she begins to cry. Mother's attention is now diverted from her friend and turns to her baby. As Mother prepares to care for her, Kathy's crying intensifies, and we hear some complaint in that crying, some impatience and anger. As Mother decides on feeding and prepares to do so, Kathy's reaction mounts further, and she is now crying angrily. If Kathy's mother were not to respond to her at this point, Kathy would probably experience excessive unpleasure.

Our aim in this chapter is to help parents prevent excessive unpleasure experiences and reduce the frequency of their occurrence. Also, since some experiences of excessive unpleasure are unavoidable, we want to help parents decrease their intensity and duration and lessen their impact.

As we have already emphasized, excessive unpleasure is necessary for the production of all forms of hostility. Thus, preventing and lessening excessive unpleasure experiences are the most direct ways of preventing the generation or mobilization of excessive hostility in the child. In doing so, parents need to know what their child's experience of excessive unpleasure looks and feels like. It is essential for them to open themselves to feeling what their child is feeling and to develop their capacities for empathy. Next, parents need to recognize that the child, especially the young child, turns to the caregiver for the relief of pain. First, the parent needs to be emotionally available and responsive to the child's need for help. Next, the parent must identify the source of pain and distress and attempt to deal with it. Finally, he or she must comfort the child during experiences of excessive unpleasure and help the child master his or her painful experiences.

Rationale

From earliest infancy on, the experience of excessive unpleasure is the prerequisite for the production of all forms of hostility, from neonatal rage reactions to later reactions of anger, hostility, rage, and hate. As we said before, preventing and lessening excessive unpleasure experiences are the most direct ways of preventing hostility in the child. Bear in mind that we are more concerned with preventing *excessive* unpleasure than unpleasure in general. Many times, unpleasure in moderate doses engenders adaptation and promotes healthy development and learning.

However, the younger the child, the less he or she is likely to be able to deal with unpleasure successfully.

Let's remember that there are times when hostility is adaptive and is needed in coping with life situations. Because of this, we do not want to—not that we could—do away with the capacity to be angry, very angry, and at times appropriately hostile and hating.

The generation of hostility in us is unavoidable, even under the best of home circumstances. For instance, growth-promoting child rearing often requires limit setting, which brings experiences of excessive unpleasure. Furthermore, life events often bring exceedingly painful disappointments and even catastrophes.

It is *excessive hostility* within the child that creates havoc. This is what we want to prevent. Preventing excessive hostility is much easier than lessening excessive hostility that has previously been generated within the child. Furthermore, lessening excessive hostility before it stabilizes in the psyche is much easier than curing or reducing stabilized excessive hostility that is embedded in the personality.

Preventing experiences of excessive unpleasure and lessening those experiences of excessive unpleasure that are unavoidable are two of the cardinal parenting activities that can lessen the chance of a child's becoming excessively hostile. The task is not easy. Because benign experiences of unpleasure lead to adaptation, to efforts toward mastery of self and environment and, therefore, are constructive, parents have to learn to differentiate between benign and excessive unpleasure. So, too, we must distinguish between benign anger and hostility and excessive hostility. Trusting one's own feelings and judgment are inherent requirements of parenting. When the child experiences unpleasure, the parent's helpful actions can be highly instrumental in lessening the intensity of the pain. They also lessen the likelihood of unpleasure becoming the usual way of experiencing specific events and life in general. They will also lessen the likelihood of hostility becoming an automatic reaction and too large a part of their child's personality.

Know What Your Child's Experience of Excessive Unpleasure Looks and Feels Like

To prevent or lessen the intensity of excessive unpleasure, parents have to know what their child's experience of excessive unpleasure looks and feels like. Just as each child has his own particular way of expressing the experience of excessive unpleasure, each child has his own threshold for experiencing pain as excessive. Children vary in such thresholds, from birth on. In addition, that threshold for experiencing pain as "too much" will vary within a given child from day to day, from morning to evening. For reasons that are not always clear to us, some days we are more easily upset than others. Many factors contribute to where our thresholds of irritability or pain tolerance may lie on any given day, at any given time. This changing threshold makes it important for parents to be able to recognize the child's communication of excessive unpleasure.

First, it is essential that parents open themselves to attempting to feel what the child is feeling. We are speak-

Excessive unpleasure generates hostility. While situations producing unpleasure cannot be completely avoided, minimizing them will prevent the generation of hostility.

ing, of course, of empathy. All parents are capable of empathy; most parents are marvelous at it. It is one of the most important capabilities required of parents to produce growth-promoting parenting. Ask yourself: "What is my child feeling right now?" There are many instances when that question ought to be asked, but a parent may be out of sorts, upset, angry with the child, and perhaps even unwilling to ask it. Nonetheless, it is essential for recognizing the experience of excessive unpleasure in the child. We cannot say too often that empathy—the ability to sense and resonate with what another person is feeling and experiencing—is a cardinal requirement for growth-promoting parenting.

Children, from very early in life, express what they feel by means of bodily and facial behaviors and the sounds they make. Their expression of feelings is most readily manifest in their faces.

Start by asking, "What is my child feeling and experiencing right now?" There are two principal ways to enhance the ability to answer that question. First, listen to the sounds the child is making. Even the newborn will make emotional sounds that are recognizable. Then look at the child's facial expression and bodily gestures. Try to guess what feelings are expressed through the sounds, the facial expressions, and the gestures. If you sounded, looked, and gestured so, what would you be feeling? This is what your child is probably feeling.

If you continue to be puzzled, try the process the other way around. How would you react—in sounds, facial expression, and body movements—if you were frightened, hurt, sad, or enraged?

Parents get to know their babies by letting themselves feel, without thinking about it, what the baby is conveying to them. For instance, when a mother feeding her baby feels her infant stop the smooth, rhythmic sucking and swallowing and notices the tensing and contorting body in her arms, her attention is quickly drawn to the baby. She will think to herself, "Oh, oh, what's going on?" Without being aware of it, she prepares to act. She will already be open to several possible courses of action and, without much awareness that she is doing so, will decide to stop the nursing, chat with the baby, place the baby on her shoulder, try to facilitate a burp, and so forth. Much of this has gone on without conscious thought, through a wide-open channel of emotional communication.

Maintaining an open channel to feeling what one's child is experiencing does not apply only to babies. Parents can also experience the feelings of their school-age and adolescent children when the children do not resist confronting their own feelings.

One of the major obstacles to empathizing is that too many parents wrongly believe young children do not feel distress and pain, or that these will not be remembered in such a way as to emotionally affect the child. Healthy development begins at the beginning, in earliest infancy—in fact, even before that. As we will insist throughout these pages, we do not want to alarm parents. Mistakes in parenting can most often be repaired. Most traumas can be mitigated and resolved. Our aim is to facilitate parenting by informing our readers, by adding to the great care and devotion they bring to their parenting work.

A note of caution: We are not recommending that parents attempt to prevent all pain, all discomfort, or all distress. In moderate doses, these experiences call for efforts by the child to adapt and develop increasingly reasonable pain and frustration tolerance, plus increased skills in coping and learning. When possible, the parents must intervene at the point when the child conveys that his feelings are becoming too difficult to bear. Again, the parents' own gut responses—their instinctive feelings—should be taken into account and trusted.

Recognize that the Child Turns to the Caregiver for the Relief of Pain

From the earliest months of life, if not, in fact, from the first days of life, infants turn to those who nurture them for the relief of pain. Recent studies have revealed that infants recognize their mother's voice, their mother's smell, the feel of their mother's body, the feel of being held, the ways their mothers and fathers hold them. They begin from very early on, not only to identify, but to respond to, the ways they are cared for, good as well as bad.

We assume that infants are responsive to the way those who care for them feel about them. They can experience being comforted, being tended tenderly, or being handled roughly or indifferently. They can tell when they are held by the one or two people who "love" them, as compared to others. All of us, from the earliest days of our lives, can feel when we are with someone who likes us and feels warmly and lovingly toward us. We can also tell when we are with someone who is indifferent to us and fails to read our wishes, our messages, and our feelings. This perception is highly influential in determining the person the child will turn to for the relief of pain. The child turns for relief to the people to whom she or he is most emotionally attached.

This has a number of advantages, including the insurance of attachment and socialization within families.

Be Emotionally Available and Responsive to the Child's Need for Help

Having empathized and sensed that the child is turning to you (even when the child's or adolescent's appeal for help is not evident or directly stated), you next need to be emotionally available. That means not only that the parent has to be present, but emotionally responsive to the infant's need for help. Although the parent may be engaged in some other activity, he or she should be ready and able to disengage from that activity and respond to the infant's appeal for help.

Parents, of course, have enormous responsibilities, and there is always too much work to do. There are times when it will not be possible for the parent to be responsive to the child's appeal. For instance, Mother may be in the middle of cooking, or writing out an idea she must commit to paper immediately, or some other activity that she cannot leave at the moment. At these times, a word that conveys the child is being heard and understood, but will have to wait a moment longer, can be helpful to the child's feeling that he has been heard and that his pain is not a matter of indifference to the caregiver. Even young infants can be asked to wait for reasonable lengths of time and can be comforted by means of the mother's voice, a glance, or other responses. If the mother is able, her response to the infant's appeal can be immediate. It is not necessary, how-ever, that parents respond with alarm or drop whatever they are doing and immediately turn to their infants when-ever the infant complains. Judgment and common sense dictate how quickly the parent needs to respond to the infant's appeal for help.

Try to Identify the Source of the Excessive Unpleasure

Next comes identifying the source of pain and distress and attempting to deal with it. Parents hardly need to be told this, because they find it quite natural to wonder "What's wrong?" As every parent knows, there are times when it is easy to identify what is wrong, and there are times when it is difficult, or even impossible. It is especially then, after many efforts do not succeed in calming a crying infant, that a parent may resort to the erroneous theory that the child cries because he needs to exercise his lungs.

Where possible, of course, once it is identified, the source of unpleasure is removed. However, there are many times when an identifiable source of unpleasure may not be entirely removable. Take, for instance, the young child who has a fever and picks at his ear, suggesting an earache. In such a situation, children of all ages become aware of the fact that the parent is trying to identify the source of unpleasure and put a stop to it. Even where the parent does not succeed in stopping the pain, the child is comforted by the fact that the parent is trying. Every parent perceives or comes to learn—except when the parent is upset—that her child feels valued when she makes an effort to help him, even when that effort does not succeed in removing the pain.

Most parents tend to comfort the child automatically, even before knowing what is causing the pain. That tendency is highly valuable, because it promotes the feeling of being valued, of being in an environment that can be helpful (even when it fails to be so). It enhances positively valenced attachment and confidence in others. When children seek comfort, a positive response is warranted. *Children do not seek comfort when they do not need it.*

The parent has an opportunity to be helpful to her child in what we in clinical mental-health work identify as "working through." Working through is a process in which an unpleasant experience—be it a trauma or an emotional conflict—is gradually dealt with in ways leading to an understanding of the nature of the trauma, reducing its impact, or resolving the conflict and rendering the experience no longer excessively painful. We speak of it as gaining mastery over an experience in which we felt helpless. This can be done by talking about what happened after the immediate experience has subsided and then talking about it again later. Where possible, it is helpful to prepare a child for an event that one anticipates may be painful by talking about it before it happens. Then, after the painful event has occurred, it is useful—especially where the child or adolescent experienced it highly painfully—to make opportunities for talking about what happened. It helps to discuss how it came about and to talk about how the child or adolescent

Nothing heals better than TLC. It also protects against hostility being generated.

felt. If it is appropriate, it helps to talk about how the child or adolescent can protect himself from being subjected to that kind of experience again. It helps just to let the child or adolescent know that experiences of this kind benefit from being talked about.

Here is an example of working through.

On the way home from a visit to neighbors who also have a 24-month-old, Mother says to 24-month-old Timmy, who seems a bit upset: "It was hard that Johnny didn't let you play with his new truck. But, you know, his daddy just gave it to him. Maybe next time you can ask him if he'll let you play with it." When Timmy responds that Johnny is bad, his mother listens to his complaint sympathetically. Then she tries to explain again that Johnny was just not ready to let Timmy play with it this time. She soothes his hurt feelings by letting him express them, by being sympathetic, and by explaining reasonably and truthfully why she believes Johnny would not let him play with his new truck.

There are, of course, much more serious issues that can benefit from talking together and working through, such as why Mother needs to leave Timmy to go to work, or why she had to go to the hospital for several days, and so forth.

When children are allowed to express their feelings and even to complain—which is usually advantageous, unless it is abused—the child may bring the subject up himself/herself for the purpose of further working through and mastering the painful experience. Usually, when children bring up an event that caused them pain, it is because they have insufficiently mastered it and want a further opportunity to do so. Therefore, it is generally useful to allow the child to talk about an event that caused pain and to help the child emerge with a better sense of being able to deal with such events. Talking to one's child about painful experiences helps him resolve the pain and acquire a feeling of being capable of mastering painful, difficult, and challenging events. We must emphasize that unresolved reactions to painful experiences continue to remain in a child's psyche and impact on that child's emotional development.

We want to emphasize that it is highly protective of the child's well-being when parents attempt to prevent experiences of excessive unpleasure where this is reasonably feasible. At the same time, we want to reiterate that parents cannot, and should not, always prevent benign experiences of unpleasure. Benign unpleasure experiences lead to adaptation and learning.

To show how early in a child's life these issues apply, consider 18-week-old Jane, reaching for a block just beyond her grasp. She reaches, strains, stops, stares at the block, readies again with effort, and groans, but can't get to it. She stops. She stares at the block again and, pressured from within, thrusts her entire body forward, brings her entire arm down, reaches the block, grasps it, and brings it to her mouth for exploration. She was frustrated by not being able to get hold of it. This produced a mild degree of unpleasure, propelling her to make the effort we saw—and she succeeded.

Think of a 10-year-old struggling to catch a ball by repeatedly throwing it in the air and catching it. Consider the 14-year-old struggling to solve an algebra problem. In addition to working because she is expected to solve the problem, she is struggling because her not knowing how to do something creates a feeling of incompetence (unpleasure) in her, and this she will not settle for!

Optimal emotional development requires both reasonable gratifications and frustrations. Parents do not need to frustrate their children in order to toughen them. Life frustrates all of us well enough, in and of itself. Furthermore, children know when they are being intentionally frustrated. This undermines the child's trusting the parent and experiencing the parent as someone he can turn to. To top it all off, it makes the child unnecessarily angry with the parent. However, we do not encourage parents to try to protect their children against reasonable frustrations. It is not desirable to protect the child against all hurt, frustration, and disappointment. "Bending over backward" is not generally helpful.

We all know it is not always possible to avoid experiences of excessive unpleasure. The important factor is that a parent's efforts to make a child feel better is never lost on a child. Experiences of unpleasure invariably make the child feel the need for soothing, for proof of being loved, and for proof of the parent's interest in and caring for the child— even when the parent's actions (or the child's experience of them) have been the source of the excessive unpleasure. We have learned that gratifying the need to be comforted within the experience of excessive unpleasure is highly growth promoting. Every parent has had the experience of a young child sustaining a benign injury, in response to which the child comes to the mother for help. Often, the mother's kissing the hurt body part, be it a finger, a hand, or a nose, may be all that is required to make the distress and feeling of hurt go away. We all know that the mother's show of tender loving care—which parents and nurses have known from the beginning of time—has magnificent pain-reducing and healing powers.

The less the excessive unpleasure experience, the better it is reduced, shortened, resolved, and worked through, the less hostility will be generated and mobilized in your child.

CHAPTER 4

Recognizing the Need for and Allowing Children Sufficient and Reasonable Autonomy

Many years ago we had the opportunity, in the course of a home visit, to observe the following situation.

A 22-month-old boy was continually being reprimanded by his mother for touching things—ashtrays, picture frames, knickknacks, a radio, a television—all of which were easily within his reach in the living room and kitchen. Mother was enormously frustrated by her child's constant need to touch things. She frequently scolded him and was constantly on her feet, pulling him away from one thing after another. Gradually the child's frustration mounted, he became angry, sulking, and a very distressing battle of wills developed between the two of them.

To a greater or lesser degree, every parent of a 1½-year-old child has somewhat similar experiences.

Parents should recognize that the development of a sense of self is propelled by strong internal forces. While the child needs to be guided in the course of development, excessive frustration of her strivings to develop a sense of self often becomes a source of heightened hostility in the child. Parents should recognize that inner pressures to act individually and autonomously are inborn. In fact, they drive the child to actions even the child herself will at times object to and be shocked by. However, the child's experience of these inner pressures needs to be protected and progressively organized by the child. The necessary guidance and protection can be provided in ways that will enhance the child's ability to be constructively assertive, while protecting against the undue generation (production) and mobilization of hostility. In order for this to occur, it is necessary to understand and respect your child's needs for age-appropriate autonomy and opportunities for exploration, while setting reasonable limits and helping the child master her inner pressures.

Baby proofing the house will prevent the unnecessary frustration of the child's explorations, the unnecessary setting of limits, and unnecessary conflicts between parent and child, all of which produce pain and heighten hostility. When possible, it is advantageous for parents to help the child in her explorations when she needs and asks for it. When it seems reasonable to the parents, it is advantageous to allow the child to learn and explore on her own, especially when that is what the child wants. Children need age-appropriate opportunities to do things on their own, in order to become independent and autonomous. Finally, it helps if parents find safe and reasonable ways to enhance the child's explorations and attempts to learn about the world and how to master it.

Rationale

Studies show that during certain periods of wakefulness from even the first days and weeks of life, infants tend to be busy exploring their surroundings. They do this visually at first, by looking about themselves. Soon, when the capability for it emerges, they begin to physically explore themselves and their environment. We consider this thrust to activity to be an effort to master one's own body and the environment into which the child is born.

As every mother of an average 1- to 2-year-old knows, there are many instances when she will have to intervene in the child's behalf because the child's explorations may lead to harm to herself, the mother, or some valued possession. Parental interventions of this kind are necessary for the well-being, protection, and socialization of the child.

From the middle of the first year of life on, parents will find that interfering with an infant's thrust toward exploring often leads to a reaction of frustration and/or anger. Where these interferences occur frequently, frustration and anger will mount. Too much frustration of the thrust to explore, of strivings toward autonomy during the first years of life, is experienced as excessively unpleasurable and generates anger and hostility toward the frustrator. It also is important to know that too much frustration of autonomy strivings—especially in the form of exploration and the mastery of self and environment—during the first years of life may interfere with the thrust to learn, the development of learning skills, and the development of intelligence.

Columbus discovered America, and Doris is discovering and exploring *her* new world.

Therefore, it is important that parents provide an environment that will allow for sufficient and reasonable autonomous activity.

What Motivates This Type of Behavior?

A number of factors operate within the infant to bring about the kind of activity we saw in the 22-month-old boy we mentioned at the beginning of this chapter. There are a number of ways of looking at it, and varying explanations have been put forward. This is ours.

From about the middle of the first year of life, the following seems to be evident in every normal child: a notable increase in energy that fuels locomotion (crawling and walking); a notable increase in interest in, and curiosity about, the surrounding environment, with an increased need to explore that environment; a notable inner pressure to move into it. We have proposed that a maturational spurt is occurring in the child, which includes an upsurge of aggression that gives character to the activities just described. This aggression is nondestructive, and it plays a critical part in the development of mastery of self and the environment. It fuels strivings toward becoming an individual and strivings toward autonomy. Furthermore, it plays a large part in learning about the self and the environment, as well as in the development of skills and adaptation.

We want to emphasize that the motivation for these activities and strivings toward autonomy arises from within the child. These inner pressures and strivings for autonomy are biological and psychological. The child is as much the victim of these inner pressures as are the objects the infant explores and may break.

In the example cited above, Mrs. Jones, like many a parent, was not aware that her young child was driven by

The sufficient play of nondestructive aggression allows for autonomy, assertiveness, and mastery. It drives kids up trees and adults up Mt. Everest.

inner forces over which he was just beginning to develop some control. Children under these conditions seem at times to behave as though someone turned a switch on. They are being driven by the released energy, and they have little, if any, means of stopping that energy from pushing them into activity. Parents commonly believe their child's inner-drivenness is intentional, something the child has control over. They see their child as willful and intentionally provocative. Surely, at some point in the course of development, every child's activity is intentional, and many a child does become willful and obnoxious. However, it is important for parents to recognize that there is a motivational force at play, over which the child, in her first part of her second year of life, has little control. Then the child needs the parent's help in developing these controls. We have found children to be occasionally bewildered by things they do when their inner-drivenness pushes them to get their hands on things around them.

One 14-month-old, in reaching for a lamp he was drawn to, pushed it as he was exploring it. His interest and curiosity changed to surprise and fear when the lamp fell with a crash. Although it did not break, the child reacted with distress and started to cry. Think also of the 18-month-old who got hold of Mother's cup of hot coffee and took a sip before Mother could get to him. His shock on contact with the hot coffee was clear. And, of course, children often react with fear when they have unexpectedly destroyed something. Although this fear at times is due to the threat of parental disapproval, the child's fear is especially due to her own feeling of losing control. With this comes the terrible fear of becoming violent and destructive of others and self.

What Can the Parent Do?

First, as we already suggested, it is important for parents to understand that the inner-drivenness we have just talked about begins to manifest itself during the middle of the first year of life. Children are truly unable to control these inner pressures at the outset. The reasonable help of their parents is required to help them gradually learn to control these pressures.

The second thing is well known to all parents and has been talked about for decades. Benjamin Spock and many other pediatricians have rightly advised parents to baby proof the house. It is possible, without making one's house threadbare and unattractive, to put breakable, valuable, and dangerous items out of the reach of children. This will facilitate the mother's care and protect the child's sense of well-being. It will provide an environment less likely to interfere with the child's curiosity, the exercise of his beginning skills as an explorer and a student of the universe in which he lives, and the development of the skills this kind of interest and exploration brings. It will decrease the frequency of experiencing excessive unpleasure and excessive frustration at the hands of a mother who is attempting to protect her valuables as well as her highly valued infant. Thus it will prevent the unnecessary generation and mobilization of hostility and make life easier for Mother and child. House proofing to match the child's developing ability to evaluate what can and cannot hurt her and her ability to control her body, as well as its inner pressures, will prevent crises which produce pain and heighten hostility.

However, as all parents know, even the best house proofing will not prevent some unpleasant encounters. Unavoidable everyday crises will result from the need to limit a child's activities, to deny a child's wish, to say no. All parents have experienced battles of wills with their infants. We will talk about handling such events and crises in the chapter that follows on setting limits constructively.

A third consideration of importance to child and parent

follows here. Much exploratory-mastery activity, school-learning activity, and development of skills be it in sports or artistic endeavors, serves strivings toward autonomy, individuality, and the development of self. At times these efforts are best exercised when the child tries things on her own. At other times, the child needs the help of a teacher, the first teacher of every child being, of course, her parent. It is enormously helpful (to both child and parent) when the parent can determine whether the child wants to "Do it myself" or wants help. Given the chance, the child will usually communicate clearly whether or not she wants help.

As in all parenting, *reasonableness* should determine the parent's behavior. If there is a risk in letting a child do what she wants—for example, the 2-year-old who wants to climb on a chair to help Mother or Father cook—it has to be disallowed. If the 9-year-old wants to help Father fix a leaking water faucet, it may take more time, but the benefits can be large to the child's feeling of competence, increasing individual skills, and relatedness to her father. If time is short, the child should be told so, and occasion taken another time to allow the parent to help the child do something she has not yet learned.

Of special importance to this issue of enhancing strivings for autonomy is to let the child do things on her own. Children need age-appropriate opportunities to be independent and autonomous. At the beginning, the parents virtually do everything for the child: make all the decisions, feed the child when she is hungry, and help her sleep when she is tired. This gradually expands to the child's letting parents know that she prefers certain foods, and later still, that she wants to choose certain clothes. Again, when it seems reasonable, children should be allowed to make independent decisions of an age-appropriate nature. Parents of young children sometimes want to help when the child may not want help or may experience the offered help as an intrusion. This causes frustration of autonomy strivings, unpleasure, and annoyance in the child, much to the dismay of the parent, who really just wanted to help. Help is great—when it is felt needed by the person being helped. Otherwise it may be experienced as interfering with the child's own efforts to master and grow. Then, the effort to help can generate hostility.

Of course, it is helpful when parents devise age-appropriate ways of enhancing a toddler's bustling curiosity and interest in the world the child is discovering day by day. It helps to recognize—especially when the child's exploratory activity becomes troublesome—that the young child (and the adolescent too) is deeply curious and interested in learning about things that are novel. She seems pressured from within to know things, in order to have a feeling of mastery over them. Finding ways to allow safe, reasonable, and supervised exploration is highly desirable from early childhood on. We believe that good learning habits begin in the toddler and may well carry into schoolwork and beyond.

Now let's talk about a major area of difficulty between child and parent, one that invariably generates and mobilizes hostility: setting limits.

CHAPTER 5

Setting Limits Constructively

Thirteen-month-old Louis reaches for an air conditioner plug engaged in an electrical outlet. What does Mother or Father do? We have seen varying reactions. One mother firmly prohibits Louis's touching the plug or outlet, getting up quickly and telling him it's a dangerous thing. He persists, and, with Mother's further prohibition, he becomes angry. She holds his hands nicely but firmly as he pulls against her effort to inhibit his reaching for the plug, and, with seriousness in her voice, she tells him he is not allowed to touch the plug or outlet because he might get hurt. She tells him she loves him and doesn't want him to get hurt. He gets angrier and begins to cry. When he then reaches for her to be picked up, she does so. While comforting him, she repeats her prohibition and the reason for it. She also tells him that she knows it's hard to not be able to do what he wants.

Another mother seeing this type of behavior at first says nothing. But as her young child persists in touching the plug, she shouts from across the room that he'd better get away from that or she'll smack him. Because he does not comply with Mother's distance communication, she goes to him, yanks his arm angrily, and loudly proclaims that he is determined to kill himself. Now frightened, he stretches his arms out to Mother. She ignores him and returns to her seat.

It helps if the parent understands that setting limits, which is often needed to protect the child against harm, confronts and stands in the way of the child's strivings for autonomy. This generates hostility in the child toward the limit setter, who most commonly is a loved parent. This brings about a conflict of ambivalence within the child, which may lead to problems in the development of autonomy and the sense of self. However, this conflict can also be helpful in the child's learning how to deal constructively with her own hostility and in developing a conscience.

It is helpful for parents to be able to distinguish between limit setting and punishment. Limit setting is the parent's acting in the child's behalf where the child cannot yet determine how she should behave or is unable to behave properly. Punishment is the withdrawal of a privilege or the inflicting of some pain to enforce, show disapproval of, and demand a price for not adhering to parental dictates.

Limits need to be set whenever they are called for, but only when truly needed: to protect the child, to protect others, to protect valued possessions, to help the child behave in a socially acceptable way. Limits need to be appropriate to the child's age, the way the child is feeling, and to the situation. Limits should be clear and understandable, with appropriate explanations and reasonable firmness. They are set to inform and guide the child. Where needed, limits should be enforced and backed up. But parents should also be able to back down on a limit they find, on reconsideration, to be unnecessary. Punish when it is absolutely necessary and after a warning has been given. However, it helps to punish with care and respect for your child. In the course of limit setting, when your child is upset and wants you to comfort her, do so. Then repeat your limit and give reasons for it.

Rationale

Limit setting invariably encroaches on the child's strivings for autonomy. Strivings for autonomy are powerful. They begin to manifest themselves with force from the middle of the first year of life, and they are driven from within. When the parent attempts to restrict the activities of a young child thrust by that inner pressure, frustration unavoidably results. Like all other forms of unpleasure, when frustration becomes excessive it generates hostility within the child. This hostility is experienced toward the person who is setting the limit. Because the person is most commonly one who is highly emotionally valued by the child—Mother—the hostility experienced is toward someone the child loves. Setting limits then, when it produces excessive unpleasure, generates hostility in the child toward the parent.

Limit setting is necessary in the face of the child's doing things that are harmful to herself, to others, or to valued things. Limit setting is also called for when a child behaves in a socially unacceptable manner. Here we mean something like the child's taking another child's toy against the latter's will. We do not mean that young children need to be compelled to say "Thank you" or "Please." This, we believe, will come by itself, if parents are polite enough with their children, their mates, their friends, attendants in stores, and so forth. Limit setting by the parent is a necessary phenomenon, that helps the child learn to behave in ways that are acceptable to the family in which she is reared.

Limit setting is difficult for parents, as well as for children. It is troublesome when setting limits that are in the child's or teenager's best interest wins hostility instead of appreciation. The reward of hostility for doing something that one feels to be helpful is invariably painful to us. What thanks for trying to help your kid! Consider the difficulty your 13-year-old daughter might encounter, were she allowed on a date with an 18-year-old boy she likes but who does not know she is only thirteen! Mother sets limits. The 13-year-old becomes furious and stomps upstairs, shouting that she hates her mother, her mother never trusts her, and so forth. It cannot be avoided. But care is needed.

In addition, the child's reaction evokes in the parent an almost unavoidable counterreaction of anger, which makes it difficult for the parent to set further limits. A parent will often avoid setting necessary limits because of the hostility they will mobilize in the child and, secondarily, in the parent. Feeling hostility toward the children we love commonly produces feelings of guilt and self-doubt, plus the feeling that one is being a hurtful parent.

Another common by-product of this state of affairs is

that parents may tend to set limits punitively and punish before it is necessary. A third common by-product is that parents may set limits and inconsistently follow through with that limit setting. That is to say, they will feel conflict over setting limits and will do so in an unclear manner, often conveying their uncertain feelings about it.

In the child, the difficulties arise because her strivings for autonomy are being interfered with. If limit setting is done in a context of overriding hostility in both child and parent, it may lead to some problems in the development of autonomy and the sense of self.

Secondly, limit setting quite commonly stirs up feelings of hostility toward the parent the child loves, thereby producing a conflict of ambivalence within the child. Ambivalence is an internal conflict produced by coexisting (or rapidly alternating) feelings of love and hate toward a valued person. It creates an internal conflict within the child. This type of conflict, by the way, is quite unavoidable in human relationships. Furthermore, feelings of hostility, and even hate, toward someone we love occurs on the part of the child toward the parent, as well as on the part of the parent toward the child.

We want to emphasize that while this kind of conflict holds the potential for creating problems within the child, at the same time, it can produce significant healthy growth. On the positive side, this conflict of ambivalence will trigger accommodative reactions on the part of the child that will lead to: learning how to deal constructively with one's own hostility; internalizing the morals and dictates of the parents; forging the quality of reasonable compliance to authority and instructors; and molding healthy assertiveness within the child.

Limit setting, then, impacts significantly on the parent and child. For both, its consequences are significant. Now let's talk about how to set limits.

Interventional Steps

Let's first understand what we mean by limit setting. Because limit setting is in the domain of discipline, it bears a relationship to punishment that needs clarification. *Discipline* is the parents' efforts to inculcate in the child behaviors that are acceptable to them and to the social group in which they live. Discipline is usually brought about when the child's behavior challenges the parents' wishes and beliefs of what the child's conduct should be. Ultimately, discipline is brought into play to tailor the child's behavior to acceptable forms. All parents hope that their children will ultimately internalize their views of what the child's conduct is expected to be.

Limit setting and punishment are both strategies employed by the parents in the service of discipline. *Limit setting* is the parent's restriction of some activity the parent feels is harmful—to the child, to the parent, to someone else, to something valued—or which is not socially acceptable. In this, the parent acts as an extension of the child's adaptive functioning, at a time when these functions are not sufficiently developed within the child. In other words, the parent does for the child what the child cannot yet do

for herself because of insufficient ability or a lack of understanding of the consequences of her actions.

Punishment is a strategy in which — as a sign of significant
disapproval and to enforce one's dictates — the parent with-
draws a privilege or inflicts pain upon the child. In the best
of circumstances where punishment is implemented, we
assume it is in the child's best interest. As all parents know,
punishment often brings with it the discharge of the parent's own hostility toward the child, which tends to dimin-
ish its aim of being in the child's best interest. Even the best
parents are at times driven to actions they regret by their
children's behavior. Children, by virtue of the large difficulties produced in them by growing up, by the demands of
the environment on them, by the occasionally excessive
demands they make on themselves, and by the significant
frustrations and pains often imposed on them by social
interaction, are highly capable at times of pushing even the
best of parents to the point where the parents behave in
ways they subsequently regret. There is no way out of it: It
will be necessary for parents to discipline their children, to
set limits, and from time to time to punish them.

In summary, limit setting is the parent's acting in the
child's behalf when she cannot yet determine how she
should behave or is unable to do so herself. Punishment is
the withdrawal of a privilege or the inflicting of some pain
to enforce, show disapproval of, and demand a price for not
adhering to a parental dictate.

We have found that because parents tend not to draw
this distinction between setting limits and punishing, they
often have difficulty setting limits constructively. They

especially avoid setting limits when their anger arouses within them the fear that they will harm the child. But if one has a clear understanding that setting limits is intended to act in the child's behalf when the child cannot yet do so herself, the fear of causing harm wanes. Then this fear is more likely to be experienced when the parent is punishing or having difficulty controlling her or his anger toward the child, rather than when setting limits. Understanding the differences among setting limits, punishing, and fearing losing control of one's own anger is clarifying and helpful in the organizing of one's parenting behavior.

Some parents are troubled by setting limits because they feel—usually because of their own experiences as children—that setting limits will encroach on the child's autonomy and inhibit the child's developing a healthy sense of self and autonomy. Such interferences occur when limits have to be set too frequently, too harshly, and invariably lead to punishment.

Every parent who has more than one child knows that children vary in how they will respond to limits. Inborn dispositions play a large part in this. So do the child's experiences. Some children are more malleable than others, who tend to resist guidance and direction. Some children will be easier than others to set limits with, and some will challenge the parents' wits, love, and fortitude. Here we are speaking about children who fall within the wide range of normal behaviors. The significantly disturbed child, or more difficult child at the farther end of the spectrum of irritability, may require more specifically tailored strategies. Some good literature, like S. Turecki and L. Tonner's *The*

Difficult Child (New York: Bantam Books, 1985), addresses this type of child.

When to Set Limits

We have often been asked, "When should I start setting limits?" The best answer we know is, "When limits are first needed."

> When Jane was 5 months old, she crawled toward Temmy, also 5 months old. In her exploratory push, Jane grabbed the toy that Temmy held. Even though we could not infer that Jane was intentionally taking something from Temmy, in contrast to her simply being attracted to the toy Temmy was holding, the group all reacted with the feeling that this should not be permitted. Jane's mother immediately responded by going to Jane, taking the toy from her, returning it to Temmy, and telling her 5-month-old daughter that she was not allowed to take the toy from Temmy.

Some parents are taken aback by the thought and wonder if it is reasonable to set limits with a 5-month-old child. We point out that if the child is doing something the parent does not approve of, then the parent ought to convey this to the child and set an *age-appropriate* and *situation-appropriate* limit. The setting of this limit was not done with anger or annoyance. It was done with an awareness that this 5-month-old had transgressed in a social situation, and since this was not desirable social behavior, it should not be allowed.

At 13 months of age, Jane seemed to constantly be propelled—as are most children at this age—to want what others had. When she wanted my coffee, I did not allow her to take it, telling her that it was hot and that coffee is not for children. After that, she turned to her mother and indicated that she wanted some juice.

At 13 months of age, Jane was not so easy with her peers. She would be demanding, pulling, holding onto things, and she would become angry. This particular morning, she screamed twice and shouted in anger at two of her young peers. She was tenaciously pursuing the purse that Temmy was holding. Temmy held on for about a minute, but Jane persisted in her demand, kept pulling, and angrily scolded Temmy, who let go of her end and began to cry.

Jane's mother intervened. Prior to her physical intervention, Jane's mother had been giving Jane instructions from a distance, telling her not to behave as she was with Temmy and raising her voice as time went by. Ultimately, when Jane pulled the purse from Temmy, Mother got up, went to Jane, retrieved the purse from her, and returned it to Temmy. As she did so, she told Jane—with some anger and some scolding in her voice—that what Jane had done was not acceptable.

We feel that limits need to be brought into play when they are called for. We find, in our years of observation, that most children begin to require limits from the time they are about 6 months of age. All mothers know that limits are, at times, called for even earlier. Our studies show (see Chapter 1) that the requirement for limits from this time on is largely the product of a psychobiological upsurge in aggressiveness in children that is part and parcel of a maturational change occurring around this time period.

We have often found that parents are frustrated by the fact that when they set limits—even with a child as young as 6 or 13 months old—they need to repeat the limits more often than they like. 13-month-old Jane's mother was annoyed by the fact that (as had been happening for four to five months) Jane did not respond to her instructions and she had to repeat her dictate a number of times. Furthermore, she was quite annoyed when it became necessary for her to go to Jane and put some force behind the dictate she was directing at her lovely daughter.

It is important to recognize that the inner pressure driving the child does not have built-in controls. The development of controls over that inner pressure can only occur over time. It will be significantly determined by the experience the child has, as well as by the degree of inner pressure her endowment brings with it. Both will produce the fact that some children need more repetition of limits than others. Because the internalization of the mother's admonitions takes time and the internal control of these inner pressures must be developed, limit setting takes time.

Parents are often frustrated by the number of times they have to repeat an admonition. It may help if parents recognize that their admonitions come in the face of the child's doing something she wants, and often seems compelled, to do. If we are honest with ourselves, we know that no one likes to be told what to do. This is so from the very beginning of life. We are all born with inner dispositions that make us want to have and do what we want. Therefore, the mother's dictates often run against not only the child's endowment and inability to know how to control her inner pressures, but also against the child's wishes, healthy narcissism, and strivings toward autonomy. For these reasons, limit setting is a long process, one that requires repetition and is often tedious for both child and parents.

One more point on when to set limits: Because limits are going to be called for many more times than is wished for by both child and parent, that it is going to be tedious for both mother and child, and because setting limits invariably brings about a conflict between child and mother as well as a conflict within the child and often within the mother, it behooves us to *set limits only when they are truly needed.* Setting limits that are not actually necessary tends to be experienced by children as oppressive. Children are eventually able to discern whether the limit imposed by the parent is really called for or not. They may not achieve that capability when they are 1 year old, but they certainly will by the time they are eight. All in all, because of the hardship limit setting produces—even though it brings many benefits to the child—limits ought to be set only when they are truly needed.

Let's assume that you set a limit and soon came to recognize that the limit was not really necessary. For example:

Mother has just told her 4-year-old he cannot play outside with the cousin he is visiting, because he will get his clothes dirty. But he is already no longer clean, and it is near the end of the day, and Mother decides it won't really matter much now. She changes her mind. She tells him that she has thought it over and it's okay to go out. He is tickled pink!

There is much to be gained by telling your child you have reconsidered the limit you just stated and find it is not necessary. Our experience is that children are invariably appreciative of a parent changing her or his mind when that change is warranted. In more than two decades of observing infants and their mothers, we have yet to see a child turn to her mother and ridicule the mother for having changed her mind. Quite invariably, we have seen appreciation on the part of the child for this kind of behavior in the parent.

How to Set Limits

We said a few paragraphs back that limits should be set in ways that are age-appropriate and situation-appropriate. They should also be state-appropriate and history-appropriate.

Regarding *age-appropriate*: One expects different responses to what we tell our children when they are 7 months, 7 years, or 14 years of age.

Regarding *state-appropriate*: A 7-month-old who bites Mother's nipple while falling asleep requires a different tone and approach to biting than the wide-awake 3-year-old who, much distressed, bites her playmate.

Regarding *situation-appropriate*: A different tone and approach is warranted when an 18-month-old takes a toy from another child than when that 18-month-old tries to pull an air-conditioner plug or walks into the street.

And regarding *history-appropriate*: What we have in mind here is this particular child's history of reacting to your limit setting. If the child is easy to set limits with, or limits are not often required, a freer hand can be allowed in setting limits—more casualness, less firmness, more time. On the other hand, if at 12 months the child persisted in getting into the closet with cleaning materials, at 18 months pulled the chair up to the stove "to cook" when you were elsewhere, and at 2 years emptied all the drawers of her dresser in the middle of the room, she will require a more patterned setting of limits. There is likely to be less time between the start of setting limits and the warning of punishment, more firmness, greater conveyance of disapproval, and if needed, more frequent punishment.

Since limits are not intended to insult or unduly restrict the child, but rather to guide and help her, it is well to make the limits clear and understandable. Asking if a child would like to do what the mother expects her to do is not a good technique. It disregards the fact that the child is motivated by inner pressures and is already doing what she wants to do. It is far better to simply, caringly, and respectfully tell the child what you expect her to do.

It is useful to draw a distinction between being firm and being hostile. Parents often confuse the two. Sometimes when limits are being resisted, firmness and angry, hostile feelings overlap. When a mother is firm in her tone, she conveys to the child that she means what she is saying. When the mother is hostile to the child, the child will feel threatened. Clarity, language that is understandable to the child, and reasonable firmness are desirable. Firmness will increase with each repetition of the dictate. When you become angry, it is good to acknowledge it and tell the child you are getting angry.

In fact, being angry when setting limits is not uncommon and, under appropriate conditions, is quite helpful. If the child resists repeated limit setting efforts or does something that frightens the parent—as when a 2-year-old runs into the street again—anger is needed to convey that you mean

A firm prohibition or reprimand stated while Mother is holding and offering to comfort her child is more likely to be heard and taken in than one that is delivered with shaming, fury, and/or rejection of the child's appeal for comfort.

what you are saying. This is no time for smiling and blandness. Anger tells the child she is going too far or doing something unacceptable, and that the parent will now take charge on the child's behalf. In reasonable doses, anger is not destructive. Hostility, hate toward our children, putting them down (depreciation), are destructive.

When limit setting is in its early stages, explain why you are setting the limit. "You can't take Temmy's toy. It's not a nice thing to do. You wouldn't like it, if she took yours." There are exceptions. A crisis situation, as when the child toys with an air-conditioner plug, calls for a rapid limit, which is then followed by an explanation. With a child whose limit-obeying history is troublesome, explanations may also follow the limit setting. In all instances of setting limits—early in its course, or after it has been effected, or even if it has to be followed by punishment—an explanation is required. No lectures are required, just a statement of the reason for the limit.

Limits should be set to inform and guide the child in her behavior, not for the purpose of letting the child know who's boss. That is experienced by the child as injurious to her self-esteem. Because that hurts, it usually generates further hostility toward the parent.

A parent is more likely to back down from following up on a limit if the parent feels guilt about what she is doing. If the parent has it clearly in mind that what is being done is truly in order to help the child, the parent is less likely to feel guilty. If a child has got you very upset, you are likely to be furious with the child and be inclined to hurt the child by showing her who's the boss. It is better to try to avoid getting too upset with your child. For a variety of reasons, that is not always possible. If you are furious with your child, let her know that, in words as well as feeling tone. Any of us can be provoked to rage by those we love. But our own hostility and rage toward our children tends to introduce guilt into our limit setting, and this in turn leads us to back down in setting a required limit.

With respect to backing up a limit or backing down on one, each may be needed at various times. If you find the limit you have set is not needed, back down. You will lose nothing by changing your mind when it is warranted. But if the limit is needed, don't back down.

The Basic Limit-Setting Model

It is commonly difficult to back up the limit you are setting. The setting of a limit and its backing up should be a more or less gradual process. How gradual depends on the child's state, age, situation, and history. Under benign conditions, one starts with a soft tone, although even there, some degree of firmness is helpful. One continues with a repetition that is somewhat firmer, somewhat more stern. If another repetition is needed, continue with yet more firmness, more sternness. A fourth intervention might require a warning that things are getting too difficult between child and Mother. A further intervention calls for specifying what the warning holds—namely, that some punishment may be necessary. The next intervention should bring with it either the parent removing the child from the area of difficulty, the restriction of a privilege, or (depending on the parent's views) a swat on the bottom.

Now, this progression of limit setting is not intended to be used every time with every child. In some cases, the progression should be shorter than that spelled out. In other cases, more time can be taken. This depends on the child's disposition, the mother's disposition, the prevailing conditions, the frequency with which limits need to be set, and so forth. Our intention is not to prescribe a rigid strategy but to illustrate that limit setting often calls for a progressive intervention: from a simple, although firm, limit setting to punishment, if needed.

The transition from limit setting to punishment occurs when the limit is not taking hold, when the child resists the parent's admonition and repeated efforts, and when the child does not respond to the warning of punishment. As with limit setting, when it is needed and punishment has been warned, follow through: punish. But even if angry, punish with care and an awareness of respect for the child. This can be done even when very angry.

With regard to the question of punishment, particularly that of a swat on the bottom, parents differ in their views. It is not necessary to resort to physical punishment. Parents who strongly disapprove of a physical mode of punishing need not resort to that method. The withdrawal of privileges can be quite effective.

For those parents who feel that a swat on the bottom is not injurious to young children between the ages of 12 months and 5 years, a moderately firm swat on a padded bottom—meaning a diapered or clothed bottom—can be quite effective. *It is inadvisable to bare the child's bottom for the purpose of a swat.* This can make the child feel humiliated. Furthermore, it may be experienced as a sexual act or attack, even by a very young child.

It is difficult for us to believe from many years of observation that there is any cause for swatting a child less than 1 year old. It is also not necessary, indeed it is inadvisable because more harm than good can come from it, to use instruments other than the palm of one's hand on a child's padded bottom, to impact effectively. If parents do not impact effectively with a swat on the bottom, they may need to examine how they are setting limits and the character of the parent–child relationship. Work at improving the quality of their setting limits and improving the quality of relationships may be what is in order. These are far better and usually lead to more successful results than increasing the levels of punishment to secure acquiescence to, and internalization of, parental standards.

Punishments that humiliate mobilize hostility. Although they may work, the price tag may be high in terms of the child's self-esteem, well-being, ultimate acceptance of reasonable limits, and development of constructive internal controls. Limits set with the phrase "You're a bad girl" are taken seriously. They can become part of the child's self-image and cause more harm than help. Even a good child sometimes does things Mother disapproves of. Shaming hurts, generates and mobilizes hostility, and often backfires.

In terms of punishment through the withdrawal of privileges, a word of caution is needed. When choosing the withdrawal of a privilege, it is well to choose a privilege the child enjoys. A child may indicate that she does not care whether or not she can watch her favorite program. Children will often say they don't care when they are trying to cope with the threat or pain of having a privilege withdrawn. Sometimes a child may say this to retaliate against the parent, to try to make the parent feel ineffectual. In withdrawing a privilege, rely more on what you know your child has enjoyed in the past and is likely to enjoy now, rather than on the child's response when a heated battle of wills is going on between the two of you.

Limit setting requires months of repetition. Where limits need to be reaffirmed, even over years, that should be done. If parents are troubled by much difficulty with limit setting, it is good to seek professional advice as to what may be going on in the child, in the child-parent relationship, and in the family.

We have to reiterate that children are constitutionally endowed with significant variations in the tendency to comply, to be malleable, and that some children tend to be more difficult to set limits with than others. Some children respond to limits with a sharp overreaction of feeling scolded and disapproved of. Limits that are too heavy-handed for one child may be too light for another. How your child responds to limits will lead you to tailor your limits accordingly. Some infants are born with a tendency toward shyness. Such children may react with withdrawal in the face of limits that they experience as too frightening. The parent's judgment, awareness and letting herself or himself feel what the child is experiencing (empathy), the child's vulnerabilities and sensitivities, and the situation, all should help the parent determine how to set a particular limit.

There are negative consequences of expecting too much cooperation from a young child. It is not desirable for a child to be easily influenced by others and quickly give up her own strivings and wishes. Children who comply too readily, who cooperate too well, often do so at the expense of their assertiveness, their sense of autonomy, and their sense of self.

On the other hand, there are negative consequences of expecting too little cooperation. A mother who gives up too soon in setting limits may not be helping her child develop the degree of internal controls necessary for reasonable adaptation to herself, others, school, and eventually work situations and the world at large.

It is also good to recognize that expectations of cooperation and compliance should vary with age. A 6-month-old or 9-month-old is not able to cooperate and comply as well as a 3-year-old. Sometimes, of course, a 3-year-old, 8-year-old, and surely an adolescent, will resist compliance and cooperation in a way that is quite appropriate for the circumstances.

Indeed, we are all much better aware now that children who are overly compliant will often be so to their detriment. They inhibit too much their nondestructive aggression, their assertiveness, their own will. In adolescence, of course, resistance to compliance is highly expectable.

Again, a parent's judgment is essential in determining whether a child's or adolescent's cooperation and compliance are excessive or whether her resistance and rejection of dictates are excessive. That judgment will also tell the parent when some resistance is warranted and when compliance is warranted. It is important to realize the helpfulness of the child's being able to assert herself and still comply. The ability to resist influence and the ability to tolerate influence, the ability to assert oneself, and the ability to yield to the argument of another person all are necessary for coping with varying life situations.

A Critical Point in Setting Limits

Two-year-old Harry once again stood up on the chair his mother had just taken him off of. Pushed to anger, Mother swatted him on the bottom and pulled him off the chair somewhat harshly. Harry, now upset and crying, stretched his arms up to his mother, clearly conveying that he wanted her to pick him up. She turned away from him with, "I told you not to stand on the chair. You're a bad boy!" Rejected by Mother, Harry shuffled across the room to his father and leaned on him. Father said, "Don't come to me. You're being bad." Harry's crying intensified, he hid his head in the sofa, and later appeared morose.

We all operate under the general principle that we want to hold on to what feels good and get rid of what feels bad. Another way of stating this principle is that we all want to take in, to internalize, that which feels good, and we all want to eject, deny, and throw out that which feels bad. For this reason, setting limits under favorable emotional conditions tends to favor the child's internalizing the dictates of the parents. The reverse—not internalizing parental dictates—holds for limits set under conditions of hostility and mean interaction.

A critical point occurs when the parent has scolded the child and the child becomes upset and turns to the parent for comforting. If the parent has gotten to the point of scolding the child—and the child has gotten to the point of being upset enough to cry, fuss, and want comforting—it is understandable that the parent is going to be angry with the child. When the child is upset, however, who do we expect the child will turn to for comforting? Of course, she'll turn to the caregiver to whom she is attached, usually the loved parent.

We have often found that some angry mothers will reject the child's appeal for comfort under these circumstances. We have been told, "She's trying to make me change my mind," or, "She's trying to butter me up." Our view of this matter is that when a child being scolded by her mother turns to the mother for comforting, the mother (or father) should accept the plea and comfort the child. The reason for this is twofold.

First, given the principle that we all want to retain what feels good and eject from ourselves what feels bad, consider the following. The mother who picks up the child who is making a plea for comforting has the opportunity to repeat her limit setting under conditions when the child is experiencing her as the comforting, loving, soothing, good mother.

Upset because Mother told her she could not take Betty's ball, 3-year-old Lucy was on her mother's lap. Mother was gently and quietly saying, "I know it upsets you that you can't have Betty's ball. But, it's hers. She doesn't want to let you play with it right now. You can't just take it from her. I can't let you do that. I wouldn't let her take your things." Mother hugged Lucy gently. Lucy still looked a bit sad. But she slowly nodded just once and stayed, comfortable, in Mother's lap for a few minutes. Then she was off, playing with Betty again.

By contrast, the parent who refuses to comfort her child, repeats the limit in anger, and often tells the child she is a bad child, is undermining her own effort to set limits and intensifying the child's feelings of hate toward her. In addition, she is intensifying her own feelings of anger toward her child.

The first scene is one that will lead to the child's internalizing the maternal dictate, because it is stated under conditions of comforting and soothing in the hands of a good mother. The second scene makes the child wish to eject what the mother is telling her, not to hear what is being said, and therefore to resist the internalization of the maternal dictate.

Of course this is a simple model; nothing in psychic life is that easy. That is to say, yes, the second child will eventually internalize the hostile mother's actions and her hostilely stated dictate. It will, however, be internalized with an overload of anger, a wish to resist it and to be rid of it, with the full play of hostility still attached to the experience. By contrast, the child in the first scene, comforted by her loving mother, has means of mitigating the angry feelings that have been generated within her.

The second reason for responding positively to the scolded child's appeal for comfort is this. In the course of development, we all start out with feelings about ourselves and others—especially our family members, most particularly our mothers and fathers. Some of these feelings are good, and some are bad. These feelings become part of the images we have of ourselves and those around us.

Mental health professionals speak of the good self, the bad self, the good mother, the bad mother. Mental health professionals assume we all form images of ourselves, which we retain in our minds and play a large part in our emotional life. The larger our feelings of love for ourselves and our mothers, fathers, and siblings, the less our feelings of ambivalence. The larger the load of generated hostility within us—the larger our feelings of self-hate, of hate toward our mothers and fathers, the larger our negative feelings of ambivalence that stabilize over time—the greater the difficulty we encounter in life. The influence of love on the one hand, and excessive hostility on the other, in the development of our relationships, our self-esteem, and the character of our consciences, is determined by the balance of these feelings within us.

This is only a partial listing of the influence of the balance of love and hostility toward the self and others. It is well-known in the mental-health field that excessive ambivalence leads to pathologic formations that can have exceedingly harsh consequences to our adaptation to life, the formation of relationships, our ability to cope, to work, and to derive gratifications.

Taking this into account, the question of trying to mitigate the play of hostility in setting limits becomes crucial. It is exactly at the point where a child who has been scolded and now wants to be comforted that the play of ambivalence can be influenced significantly. For this reason, especially but not only in the course of setting limits, when your child pleads for comforting, pick her up, comfort her, then (when setting limits) repeat the dictate, explaining why you are stating the dictate and that you expect the child to comply with it.

CHAPTER 6

Teaching the Child to Express Hostility in Reasonable and Acceptable Ways

"It's not okay for you to hit me!" 2-year-old Jane's mother half shouted at her. "If you're mad at me, tell me. But you are not allowed to hit me!" Jane smirked, but soon seemed to feel subdued and duely scolded.

When 16-year-old Mike's mother told him he could not make a phone call just as the family was about to sit down for dinner, he stormed "What the fuck is this! You're not at the table yet!" His mother, showing feelings of being offended, said, "Don't talk to me like that. I know you're mad, but you can find a better way to let me know that than by acting like some foulmouthed kid!"

Since the generation and mobilization of hostility in children is unavoidable, all children have to be helped to find reasonable and acceptable ways to express these feelings. The generation of hostility is a cumulative phenomenon; when it is not appropriately and constructively dealt with by the child, it accumulates, stabilizes, and becomes patterned within the personality. This can interfere with all areas of a person's life. It falls to the parents to help their children learn how to cope with hostile feelings before they accumulate, become excessive, and stabilize within the child. We want parents to recognize that, unpleasant as it is when our children are very angry with us, are hostile to us, this is an opportunity to help them learn to express these feelings. We can show them ways that will not produce undue guilt in them, make them fear their anger, inhibit their assertiveness and healthy competitiveness, or hinder their learning and striving toward their personal goals.

When your child is angry, let him know that some hurt is causing his anger. Help your child find acceptable ways to verbalize feelings of hostility and hate. Tell your child that he can tell you what he is feeling and thinking, but words and intonations that are insulting or intolerable will not be allowed. Discharging hostile feelings by striking out physically is not desirable, except under particular circumstances; for example, in response to continuing bullying or an attack by someone else. Make clear that although your child can tell you whatever he feels and thinks, he is not allowed to strike you or himself. Then let your child know the reasons for this prohibition, which include: "I love you, and I don't want you to hurt me or yourself"; "Hitting me or saying foul things to me will make you feel you are bad, and will make you feel guilty."

Rationale

Many people hold the view that being angry or feeling hostile within the family is bad. Many parents ascribe anger and hostility to some "evil" tendency within the child. In both our clinical and observational work, we invariably find that hostility is reactive to traumatizing life experiences. We find no evidence that children are born with an "evil" tendency in them.

The thesis we hold — that hostile feelings are mobilized by experiences of excessive unpleasure — gives us a different picture. It means that any human being, if subjected to sufficient excessive unpleasure, will become hostile. This is particularly so early in life. Before the child is capable of sublimating feelings of hostility and dealing with them in constructive ways, hostility will be expressed in ways that are noxious to others and the self. Civilizing primitive, obnoxious tendencies in children lies in the hands of the parents, and one of the principal areas where that civilizing is needed is in dealing with hostile feelings.

If parents understand that when children are hostile it is because they have suffered excessive pain and unpleasure, they will be more sympathic. They will deal with the child's hostility more constructively and help the child deal with it more constructively.

It is essential that parents know their children need help in learning to cope with their own hostility and in finding appropriate and acceptable ways of discharging these feelings. Many well-meaning parents disapprove of all signs of anger from their children, let alone hostility and hate — especially when these are directed toward the parents. Commonly, when a 2-year-old says to his mother, "I hate you," many a mother is likely to reply, "I know you don't mean that." Indeed, the child means exactly that.

A number of problems follow from this mother's intervention. Among other things, the child feels that he is not supposed to feel what he is feeling. The child is told to disavow the feelings he knows he is experiencing. He overtly agrees with Mother, but feels he is a little monster, since he knows very well he is hating. The child's proper evaluation of what he is experiencing is undermined, and this may lead to confusion. He may come to believe that feelings he has are unacceptable, and set himself the task of denying feelings—which, in such instances, is an undesirable way of coping. This is an incomplete listing of the unfavorable consequences of not allowing a child to experience his feelings, whatever they are. When your child is angry with you, you have an opportunity to help the child deal with such feelings constructively.

There is a further consequence of the parent's disallowing that the child hates his mother. Children themselves label feelings of anger and hate as being bad. They do so sometimes even in the face of parents' telling them otherwise. Children are the first to judge themselves bad when they experience hostility toward the parent they love. This is because feelings of hostility toward those we love creates within us a profound reaction of disapproval that often may lead to self-accusations and self-hate, which we all know as guilt. A child needs the opportunity to resolve these feelings of ambivalence that produce guilt, because they can lead to the development of too harsh a conscience. So when a parent cannot tolerate the thought of the child's hating her, a thought difficult to hear to be sure, she denies the child an opportunity to deal with these feelings of hate constructively—a process in which the parent can have meaningful input.

It is not our intention to be alarming. However, it is useful for parents to know that insufficiently worked through feelings of hostility toward those we love produce all kinds of emotional disturbance and misery in people. Such feelings cannot be worked through unless they can be acknowledged, given reasonable ways of expression and discharge, and be reasonably dealt with.

In this task, the young child needs the help of his parents. Psychotherapists affirm that the great facilitator of working through feelings of hostility is to be given permission to verbalize them in the context of a meaningful, valued relationship. In the young child, the best relationships available to him are the ones with Mother and Father. Siblings can also become meaningful facilitators of the working through of overloads of hostility, although they also can become the victims of that hostility. Our aim is to help mothers, fathers, and their children develop an emotional dialogue with one another in which anger, hostility, and hate can be talked about meaningfully in a hostility-reducing way.

Interventional Steps

When the parent sees that the hostile feelings her child is experiencing are the product of some excessive unpleasure experience, she can frame her interventions in that context. A mother conveying to her child that she knows something is hurting him (be it something physical or emotional) gives him an experience that is vastly more growth promoting than hearing that he is being bad. To convey to the child that some hurt is causing the child's anger rather than that some inner evil core is at work in him, makes for an interaction of large beneficial consequence to the child's perceptions of himself, of his mother and eventually of others, and to his well-being. It frames the child's experience in a highly positive quality of human relatedness.

Another thing this reaction will do is make it less threatening and noxious for the child to experience the feelings

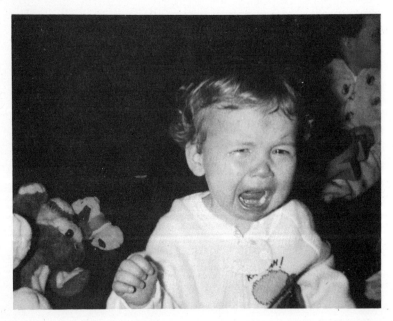

Put yourself in her place. What do you feel? How can she be helped to express her angry feelings in reasonable ways?

he is having. This helps the child to deal with them, and will open the possibility for him to verbalize what is causing his feelings. Consider the atmosphere for a dialogue between yourself and your child when you tell him he is being rotten again. Now compare that to telling your child caringly that you know something is hurting him and you would like to know what it is.

Parents can most fruitfully help a child deal with his feelings of hostility in acceptable ways when these ways emerge in the context of their own relationship. We have said many times that even the best of parenting cannot prevent numerous experiences of excessive unpleasure. The generation and mobilization of hostility within family life is unavoidable. Let's take up again the example we talked about earlier: the unpleasant and at times difficult task of setting limits with one's beloved child.

In this case, the caring parent is the instigator of the unpleasure experienced by the child and, therefore, of the child's hostility. We draw attention to the important but difficult fact that *the person the infant first hates is the infant's emotionally valued caregiver, most usually, the mother.* The reason is that it is at the hands of the responsible and loving caregiver that the child's first experiences of interactionally produced excessive unpleasure occur.

In general, the mother, the most marvelous of caregivers, unavoidably becomes the first frustrator of her child. (If the father is prominently engaged in caregiving to his infant, the same will apply to him.) Therefore, because the mother is the first frustrator of her child, she becomes the first toward whom the child's feelings of hostility and (later) hate become directed. Difficult as this is for parents, it may, in fact, be most opportune. After all, no one will be as caring in helping a child learn to cope with his hate than a loving parent. Who else is going to be willing to be subjected to a child's hate?

Twelve-month-old Mary is constantly reaching for cups, ashtrays, and other children's toys. Repeatedly, she wants to push the toy cart, which her mother has prohibited her from doing. She repeatedly goes into the hall, where her mother feels it is not safe for her to be alone. When Mother follows her into the hall, picks her up, and tells her she is not to go out there, Mary complains angrily. Her face flushes, her muscles tense, and, shaking, she yells. It is not difficult to see that she is highly frustrated and very angry with her mother. She does not hit her mother, the object of that anger; in fact, she seems at one moment to lightly hit herself in the nose. She strikes the couch and the toy cart.

At 13 months, her reactions to her mother's limit setting reach a further level. When her mother brings Mary back from the hall the first several times, Mary smiles and permits herself to be passively returned to our infant area. But then she complains more and more vigorously and vocally, contorting her body to extricate herself. Eventually she cries angrily, makes kicking motions toward her mother, and twice actually hits her mother with her arm. Once she also strikes herself.

How does one deal with that? First of all, once Mother has determined that a limit is warranted, it is important she stick to it. When Mary vocalized her anger at her mother, Mother felt embarrassed, because we were observing them.

Although she was stung by the feelings expressed by her baby, she did not stifle the child's expression of feelings. When a child cries and seems to curse at her mother (even before she has learned to use words), clearly expressing feelings of anger, the child is choosing a pathway that facilitates dealing with her feelings of anger. Therefore, it is best not to prohibit the child's crying, nonverbal "cursing," and protesting.

When we think of helping our children verbalize their feelings of anger, hostility, and hate, we have to distinguish between words that hurt and words that insult. While we want to encourage our children to verbalize difficult feelings, we do not want them to go beyond certain reasonable bounds of what one can say to another person, particularly to one who is valued and loved.

We draw the distinction by saying that parents should not tolerate words that insult, but should allow words that may hurt without insulting. We have found that some parents find certain words intolerable, whereas others do not. Perhaps "intolerable" is a dimension we should add to words that insult.

Not only are we sensitive to certain words, but we are also sensitive to the tone in which words are expressed. The tone often carries the emotional quality or the affective coloring of the feelings expressed. In helping a child verbalize feelings of hostility and hate, a boundary must be drawn. Words and intonations that are insulting or intolerable should not be allowed.

For instance, a young child's outburst of "I hate you" is undoubtedly going to hurt the mother. However, even in its most deeply felt intonations, it cannot be construed as an insult. A parent may find the words painful, yet they should not be disallowed. This example shows how difficult it is to state where to draw the line in allowing a child to verbalize feelings of hostility and hate. We each need to draw our own lines. But we have to bear in mind that it is necessary, in order to help our child, to find a range of expression that is permissible. Otherwise, there will be no verbal pathway to the resolution of hostility, which can only lead to problems. For instance, this author would distinguish between his son's calling him "a jerk" versus "a bastard" or "a son of a bitch." To be called a jerk by one's own son is a distasteful event. To be called a bastard or a son of a bitch is not acceptable to this parent.

In fact, we are talking about a far-reaching aspect of how to get along with someone one values and loves. How to fight and argue with those we love is a challenge to each of us. It certainly is a challenge to children. It is good when arguing (whether with loved ones or otherwise), to learn reasonable rules. For instance, even in boxing, there are rules: at all times, no blows below the belt. We might use that model to draw the line between words that are hurtful and words that are out of bounds, inappropriate, insulting, and intolerable.

As we have said, we often find parents upset by their children's expressions of anger. They often tell the child not to be angry, that it is bad to be angry, and—most unproductive of all—that the parent will give the child something to be angry about! In general, a young child's exclamations of anger, as when 13-month-old Mary had "had it" with her beloved mother, are desirable means of expressing what the child is feeling. It is helpful, of course, for the mother to recognize that the child is reacting to something Mother is doing to her. Then the anger being directed toward Mother cannot be surprising.

Mary kicked her mother from a distance and twice actually struck her mother in the arm. Once she struck herself. Discharging hostile feelings by striking out physically is usually not desirable. There are times, however, when a child's physically striking out is warranted, particularly when it is in response to continued bullying and/or attack by someone else. Every parent knows that bullies will not stop being bullies until the victim strikes back. There are variations to this thesis, but it is a commonly found phenomenon.

However, discharging feelings of anger by striking out physically is generally not the best way to deal with one's feelings. Striking out at the mother brings with it an added dimension: the feeling that one is being bad. This feeling will be experienced by the child even when she does not strike out at the mother, by virtue of her feeling anger toward the mother she loves.

By virtue of its being a physical act, striking at one's mother produces a double jeopardy. It is generally more difficult to reverse an act than a verbal statement. Also, an act tends to be more hurtful, more unacceptable than angry words. Given the type of circumstance we are discussing now—Mary's having a fit in response to her mother's limit setting—the adage "sticks and stones can break my bones, but words will never harm me" tends to have merit.

It is our impression that children tend to feel more guilty when they physically strike out at their parents than when they say "I hate you." We find it useful, therefore, to tell parents not to let their children strike them. Tell your child that he can say what he feels and thinks, but he is not allowed to strike you.

For the child who persists in striking out at Mother, setting limits on that act becomes necessary. It is a worthwhile project. In setting limits on the child's striking out at the mother, the strategies proposed in the chapter on setting limits should be brought into play. When the limits do not work and Mother has to resort to punishment, we tend to advocate either the withdrawal of a privilege or, in a preschool child where the parent is comfortable with doing so, a swat on the clothed bottom.

We do not feel that doing to the child what the child is doing to the parent is as desirable as withdrawing a privilege or, with a young child, administering a swat on the bottom. For example, with a young child who bites, biting the child in return is not a desirable form of punishment. A swat on the clothed bottom, by a parent who is comfortable doing so, is more educational than retaliatory, and tends to produce less fear, unpleasure, and hostility.

Just as the mother should prohibit the child's striking at her, so should the mother prohibit and protectively disapprove of the child's striking herself, as Mary did. Parents will commonly find that children (even less than 1 year of age), when excessively angry, will not only lash out against others but also against themselves. In very young children, this may occur as a result of insufficient differentiation—

not knowing who is themselves and who is the person instigating the experience leading to rage.

Even in children just around 1 year of age, when there is an acute hostility overload, the child may restrict himself from directing his hostility toward Mother or Father. Even this young, hostility toward those to whom the child is attached creates internal conflict. The alternative frequently used by young children is to direct the hate away from the valued and needed parent and turn it toward himself.

We find that children often tend to use the same reactions over and over. Thus the parent can recognize the pattern the child uses to deal with hostility overload. Parents will recognize it if their child tends to direct his hostility against himself as a selected way of dealing with hostility overload. As patterns of hostility expression and discharge are tried by the child, parents can intervene to discourage those that are undesirable.

Three-year-old Phyllis seemed somehow to get bruises, scratches, or cuts on her arms, legs, or face. We had noticed that she would fall or bump into chairs, even though she was not a clumsy child. We soon came to see that when she got upset with her younger sister and teased or hit her, and her mother would then scold her, Phyllis would scratch her own arm or bite her own hand. We inferred that she did this because she was unable to find reasonable ways to express her angry feelings. When this was drawn to the mother's and Phyllis's attention, she began talking about her feelings in a matter of a few weeks. The physical attacks on herself began to decrease and eventually stopped.

Parents are aware that directing the hate we feel toward others against ourselves is an unfavorable way of dealing with hostility. We all have seen people who cannot let themselves succeed in life because of a profound inner need to punish themselves. This is not an uncommon condition. It is important that, just as parents will not allow their children to lash out at others, they also do not allow them to lash out against themselves. This includes commonly seen behaviors such as hitting oneself, biting oneself, striking one's head against a wall or another hard object, such as a table. All of these may begin even before the end of the first year of life. In children 2 to 3 years of age and older, this can manifest itself in more hidden behaviors, such as frequently falling or getting scratched or hurt in one way or another.

Restrictions on lashing out against Mother, as well as against the self, should take essentially the same form. First comes the prohibition against doing just that. Second is a comment as to the reason for that prohibition, which is invariably in the form of: "I love you, and I don't want you to hurt me or to hurt yourself." Third, if this type of behavior has been going on for some time, point it out to the child, explain that you disapprove and expect the behavior to stop.

Again, the child's lashing out against himself may require the setting of limits. Where these fail, some benign form of punishment—such as the withdrawal of a privilege—may be required. And where this does not work, some professional help may be warranted. Let us again underline that excessive lashing out against others, as well as against the self, are unsatisfactory ways of coping with hostility overload and may lead to significant problems, both in terms of one's relationships and of one's achievements in life.

Here is another factor that parents may find supportive of their efforts to help their children learn to discharge hostility overload in constructive ways. Most parents don't need this encouragement, but it may help. When children are not helped with the expression and discharge of their hostility overload against Mother or against themselves, the child does not feel protected against his own hate reactions and desires to destroy. He becomes afraid of his own rage. This can have large negative effects on the child's development.

For instance, being afraid of one's own feelings commonly leads to the suppression or denial of those feelings. An effort is made to hide them or deny they exist, and they are stored within the self. Or the child may simply inhibit the manifestations of these feelings, blocking their reasonable expression and discharge, which intensifies their internal accumulation. Both of these reactions may lead to the freezing of one's emotional life or the inhibition of showing feelings, including not only those of hate, but also those of love, affection, and sexual gratification. Inhibitions of this type also lead to inhibitions in learning, and may eventually create school and work problems.

Here is an example of what we have found many times.

A 6-year-old boy is surprisingly quiet when with grown-ups, even with his father. He tends not to talk to them, even at times when it is expected (as with a teacher in class).

He tends to talk most easily with his mother. He does well with peers. He also is subject to temper tantrums that distress his parents greatly, and he is most enraged with his younger brother, who seems to be a source of much difficulty for him. Because he has not yet learned to control his rage well enough and is in constant dread of its bursting forth, he has to set a clamp on his feelings. This leads to inhibitions, of which talking with grown ups other than his mother is but one.

Our intention is not to alarm parents. It is to point out to them the enormous opportunity they have to help their children in the very difficult task of coping with their feelings of anger, hostility, and hate overload. Many children are bewildered by their feelings of hate and hostility against the parents they love. Mental-health professionals identify these as conflicts due to ambivalence. Ambivalence is difficult for all of us to cope with, and parents who are aware of this fact can do a great deal of prevention work in helping their children cope with their own hostility.

One other instance warrants comment. We have at times seen a 16-month-old child bump into a chair because he was not looking where he was going. In response to the child's being upset by this, a mother may say "Bad chair." There are troubles with this type of problem solving. Clearly the chair did not walk up to the child and strike out at him. The accident occurred because the child was inattentive to where he was going. It is better to help the child's evolving sense of being someone who can initiate things, someone who is responsible for his own actions. "Watch where you're going. Be careful" is far superior to "Bad chair!" Here's an important issue: Blaming an innocent object facilitates a highly problematic mechanism of dealing with one's hostility and hate. We call that mechanism *displacement*.

Displacement is a mechanism whereby, when the child is confronted by hostility overload toward a person he loves and it stirs internal conflict, as early as the first year of life, the child may elect to displace the hostility onto something or someone else. To clarify, let us return to an instance already mentioned.

Fourteen-month-old Jane was having a difficult time with her mother this morning. In the midst of one of their mild but then frequently occurring battles of wills, Jane picked up a small wooden block, raised her arm, and turned to her mother somewhat defiantly. Mother was looking at Jane quite sternly, and although she said nothing, her expression was clearly a statement of prohibition. Jane's arm came forward, and as it did so, she rotated her body slightly and threw the block at Mrs. G., who was sitting next to her mother.

We inferred from this that Jane's target was her beloved mother, but the prohibition from her mother and from within herself led Jane to displace her attack onto an innocent bystander, Mrs. G. We have extrapolated from such events that displacement is a self-protective coping mechanism implemented by all human beings to discharge hostility toward someone we love through discharging it against someone who is less important to us. This hostility discharge creates less conflict for us because that person is not as valued as the loved one.

We have concluded that displacement is a mechanism employed in what eventually becomes bullying, scape-goating, and even prejudice. In all these instances, someone other than the person toward whom the rage and hate was initially experienced has become the recipient of that rage and hate through displacement.

Therefore, blaming an innocent thing or person for hurt and hostility is an undesirable way of helping one's child solve any problem. It enhances the use of displacement in dealing with hostility overload. False blame also encourages the child to avoid dealing with situations realistically, which can only complicate a child's life. It is more to the child's advantage to learn to watch where he is going than to encourage the assumption that chairs magically move. Blaming chairs distorts facts, encourages frightening magi-cal thinking—which all children experience, even into elementary-school years and later—and interferes with the child's developing healthy adaptative precaution and rea-sonable self-care.

Like limit setting, learning how to control one's anger and hostility and to discharge it in healthy ways requires time and repeated efforts on the part of the parent. This continues into the elementary-school years and at times into adolescence. It is well to bear in mind that there are ways of discharging one's hostility in graduated doses and in ways that are tolerable to both the self and the target of one's anger. Verbalization of one's hostility in a positively meaningful relationship allows for the lessening of its accumulation in the psyche and prevents its coloring the personality. It also facilitates the development of internal controls over how one discharges hostility and hate, a process that develops gradually, with much help from parents. As with limit setting, teaching children to verbalize hostility often requires repetition to gradually effect a working through of feelings of pain (unpleasure) and mobilized hostility.

Let's go back for a moment to the example of the 2-year-old who, upset and hurt, says to his mother, "I hate you!" "Oh my," mother could say, "I'm sorry you're so mad at me now. Phew! I'm glad you don't feel this way often. You know, sometimes I get pretty mad at you, too. And I'm glad that I can think of all the times you've said you love me." Too much to say to a 2-year-old? Absolutely not.

The parents' efforts to develop, maintain, and enhance a positive dialogue with their child—which can be put into play even when dealing with angry feelings and hostility—not only provides a vehicle for the working through of painful experiences, hostility, and hate, but also secures the vehicle for healthy development in the child, including the formation of good relationships and heightened well-being. We can also toss into this promise the idea that if parents want their child to talk to them when they become adolescents—something that is not guaranteed in all families—they must talk and listen to their child and encourage their child to talk about feelings and experiences from toddlerhood on.

CHAPTER 7

How to Handle Rage Reactions and Temper Tantrums in Growth-Promoting Ways

This was just too much! Life seemed unbearable. Thirty-month-old Andy had been cranky all morning, Mother told us. In fact, he had been short-fused for several days, since Father had gone on a business trip. Just having been pushed down by 3-year-old David and now Mother telling him he couldn't have the book Susan is holding, seemed to be the straw that broke the camel's back! His distress and anger crossed the bearable line, and he fell apart. Andy was a quick reactor. We could see it coming. He had been cranky for some time and had been on the point of tears when David pushed him. Now, he burst into tears, crying angrily, and fell to the floor thrashing—in utter pain, helplessness, and rage. Mother was mortified. *Not again! In front of all these people* (a parent–infant group)!

As Andy was thrashing and screaming, Mother tried to quiet him. She seemed to feel terrible, both for him and for herself. How could she stop him from being so miserable and embarrassing them so? Andy's entire repertoire of tantrum activity—his face and sounds, especially—revealed acute pain, rage, disorganization. He appeared bewildered. After two minutes of screaming and thrashing, he seemed to lose steam, his activity slowed, and he quieted. He looked pale, washed-out, wounded. Mother had stopped half shouting at him to stop his screaming. If she could have done so without risking further humiliation, she would have walked away, gone to the bathroom, maybe, just to hide and prevent herself from smacking him. She was pale, tremulous, and hurt. Both were quiet.

Two minutes passed. Andy started to fuss again, spontaneously. Worried, Mother told him he'd better stop fussing! Andy's fussing intensified, and in a few seconds, he was into a tantrum again.

We want to explain the features inherent in temper tantrums, those that allow for intervention and those that do not, and how to lessen their intensity and duration so parents can develop better strategies for their prevention and management. We feel this will help parents lessen the frequency, intensity, and duration of temper tantrums. This is important to accomplish, because temper tantrums are traumatic for children and parents. Because it induces excessive fear and pain, a tantrum generates further hostility. Parents' efforts in helping their children deal with temper tantrums can bring enormous dividends. Temper tantrums ought to be dealt with as soon as they emerge, and are to be avoided where possible, without making oneself hostage to a child's fits of temper.

Temper tantrums have a structure. A tantrum has a beginning, mounts, reaches a peak or climax, then gradually wanes and dies down. In addition, tantrums tend to occur in waves. At the beginning of a tantrum and between outbursts of rage, an infant may be accessible to parents' interventions. However, at times of mounting distress and at the height of distress, the child is often inaccessible to external intervention.

During tantrums, it is important that the parent be near and be available to the child. Offer comforting when the rage reaction seems to be subsiding, especially when the child signals that she wants help. Don't give up if your effort to comfort is rejected, and try not to get too angry with the child. After the tantrum has subsided, talk with your child about the events that led to the tantrum and about the necessity for learning to deal better with them.

Rationale

A temper tantrum is traumatic. It is traumatic for the child, and it is traumatic for the parent.

A temper tantrum is a reaction in which the child suffers an extreme amount of excessive unpleasure. It is a generalized and diffuse rage reaction, wherein the boundaries between oneself and others fade, during which an inner sense of disorganization and helplessness prevails. All of these cumulatively cause intense pain, bewilderment, fear of disorganization and, at intervals, a loss of touch with reality. This state of experiencing occurs even in children under 4 to 6 months old. Indeed, it is more likely then, because differentiation of self and others, testing of what is really happening, and higher levels of psychic organization are not yet possible.

The traumatic effect of a tantrum does not just stay with

Big brother always ruins everything. Unbearable feelings are evident in Marc's face, the face of the tantrum about to erupt.

the child during its actual occurrence, but is re-experienced repeatedly as the child attempts to master the trauma.

In addition, by virtue of their being traumatic and inducing excessive fear and pain, temper tantrums in and of themselves generate hostility within the child. That is, a tantrum generates further hostility simply by its having occurred. Therefore, the generation of hostility arising within and from a tantrum does not stop after the temper tantrum has subsided.

Clinical evidence leads us to assume that experiences such as temper tantrums are retained in the psyche, where they maintain an undermining influence on well-being.

The strength of this influence depends on the intensity, frequency, and duration of these experiences. We have had the opportunity, in working clinically with adults, to learn about the unfavorable and sometimes long-lasting consequences of having experienced temper tantrums harshly during childhood, especially when they continued from the first years of life through early elementary-school years.

Again, we want to underscore that our aim is not to alarm parents. Rather, it is to encourage parents not to take tantrums lightly—which most do not, anyway—but at the same time, not to let tantrums intimidate them. Parents' efforts to help their children deal with temper tantrums can bring enormous dividends, both to the child and themselves. As we noted, and as every parent knows, temper tantrums not only hurt the child but are also experienced by the parent with much distress, bewilderment, embarrassment, and helplessness. A child's tantrums can be a singular factor in making a parent dislike, resent, and distance herself from her own child. Consequences to the parent are also very painful.

For these reasons, we feel that temper tantrums ought to be dealt with as soon as they emerge and are to be avoided where possible, without making oneself hostage to a child's fits of temper. We therefore want to pay special attention to them.

Interventional Steps

Let's talk about certain features of temper tantrums that are relevant to when and how to intervene with them. Many children, like 30-month-old Andy, are quick temper-tantrum reactors. Others will have temper tantrums very infrequently, and when they do occur, they occur gradually and are easy enough to deal with.

In the first type of child, the temper tantrum may occur explosively, with little warning. However brief the warning time may be, though, there are always signs of an imminent tantrum. In fact, we were not surprised when Andy's tantrum occurred, because he had been cranky for an extended period of time. He had reacted with anger which he contained when pushed by David, and his mood seemed to suggest a storm brewing. It behooves the parent to learn the particular signs her child gives off before the point of eruption.

Temper tantrums have a structure. Even in children whose temper tantrums seem to emerge suddenly, like Andy, for the most part, one can see the following structure in them. A temper tantrum has a beginning, mounts, reaches a peak or climax, then gradually wanes and dies down. This major curve (see Diagram A) occurs in all tantrums.

Let's take the example of a 6-week-old infant having signaled the need for food. Delays are at times unavoidable where bottles are used, or even when the baby is breast-fed. However, this delay was too long for this infant today. By the time Mother gets to the infant, she is in the throes of a primitive tantrum.

Commonly, a mother finds that when she attempts to put the nipple in the mouth of an infant screaming from

DIAGRAM A

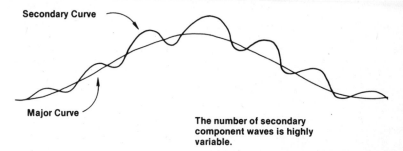

Secondary Curve

Major Curve

The number of secondary
component waves is highly
variable.

Diagram A.—A full tantrum usually mounts gradually, reaches a peak
and runs out in exhaustion. This is its major curve. But when fully
developed it is not a continuous outburst. It consists of episodic bursts
of bewildering rage and despair. These episodes can be said to consti-
tute a secondary curve riding on that of the total tantrum experience.

hunger, her attempts will not succeed at the height of the
infant's screaming fit. Every mother knows there will be a
delay in the child's ability to respond to the presentation of
the nipple. Often a mother will gently rub the nipple on the
6-week-old's lips, sensing that the child's attention has to be
brought to the nipple, in order for the tantrum to stop and
the feeding process to become possible. What is happening
here, is that under conditions of the rage reaction, the
infant cannot perceive that the environment is now making it possible for feeding to occur. It is as if the environment is tuned out, and can be tuned in only when the rage
reaction has sufficiently toned down. The rage reaction
makes the infant blind and insensitive to the possibility of

gratifying the need that started the tantrum in the first place.

Observing infants closely, be they 6 weeks or 3 years old, a parent will note that temper tantrums tend to occur in waves. That is to say, the first signs of a tantrum may be a mild wave of distress expressed in a mild episode of angry crying. This is then followed by a quieting that soon yields to another wave of crying and angry feeling. Waves of this kind increase in intensity until a tantrum becomes continuous, much stronger, and more difficult to subdue.

In other words, superimposed on the major curve of a tantrum is a secondary curve constituted of waves of tantrum episodes which, as they climb the major curve, become more and more intense (see Diagram A).

Let's look at the structure of the secondary curve with its component waves that ride on the major curve. Each of the waves in the secondary curve consists of a climbing (up) limb, a crest, and a down limb (see Diagram B).

During the climbing (up) limb, the rage reaction is accumulating in intensity and the child then is often inaccessible to external intervention. The reason is that once the limb is set in motion, the infant's ability to respond to external stimuli seems to be overwhelmed by the internal momentum of the rage being experienced.

During the crest, there is some stabilization of the rage reaction and a beginning ability to be responsive to both internal and external events.

It is, however, during the down limb that the infant is most able to hear and perceive external events, because, we

DIAGRAM B

COMPONENT WAVE OF SECOND CURVE

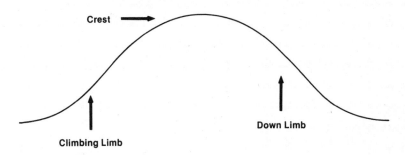

Diagram B. — Each episodic burst in the tantrum has a climbing limb, a crest, and a down limb. The child's ability to perceive external stimuli is lowered during the climbing limb and he is then usually difficult to reach emotionally. Efforts to calm then will be frustrated. Calming and helping the child pull himself together are better achieved during the down limb.

assume, the internal overtake of rage experiencing is lessened.

We have found, over years of observing tantrum reactions, that parents' efforts to intervene and comfort the infant at the very beginning of the climbing limb can work. Once the climbing limb is set in motion, however, it is too late to intervene helpfully. Perception of external events tends to be diminished, and the momentum of rage discharge is too difficult to master. This means that after amoment in the climbing limb, the parents' efforts are not likely to be heard. The best the parent can do then is prevent the infant from hurting herself, hurting another (usually the mother), or breaking things by thrashing about. Generally, during this interval of time, it is best to allow the child to thrash on the floor and protect her from harm. Taking hold of a child who is thrashing about in the course of a tantrum, a restraining maneuver that is some-times warranted, rarely applies to children under 3 or 4 years of age.

During tantrums, it is important that the parent be near and be available to the child, especially for children 4 years of age or less. This is true even for children older than that. We will comment about when to send the child to her room. In the course of the child's thrashing about, the parent should not let the child strike her in any way. If the child does so, a firm prohibition is needed. In order for this prohibition to reach the child, it will have to be firm enough and loud enough to cross the barrier to incoming external stimuli. Usually it is not advisable to leave the child who is having a tantrum, especially one less than 4 years old. This is because feeling abandoned—of which the child will become aware as soon as the crest of the rage reaction begins its down climb—while in the throes of feeling disorganized, helpless, and bewildered by internal rage, can be even further traumatizing. (See below for an exception to this recommendation.)

In the course of our analyzing a young woman, one traumatic event that was recalled again and again was that of her mother walking out of a store and leaving her—then 7 years old—momentarily behind when she had a tantrum.

When she came out of her disorganizing rage reaction to find that her mother was gone, she was mortified. Much rage and despair was attached to the fact that her mother had left her. For this reason, leaving a child who is having a tantrum is not the most constructive way of dealing with it.

Let us repeat that at the point where the climbing limb begins to be manifest, when the parent first sees signs of the emerging wave, she can at times help with a mixture of verbalized concern, warmth, and firmness. "Come on, dear, get hold of yourself. I know you're feeling awful right now!" The parent ought to offer comfort, even if the child may not be able to accept it. All in all, during the climbing limb of the rage reaction, and when the reaction is at its crest, the best one can hope to do is a holding maneuver.

The parent can be most actively helpful during the down limb of the component wave of the rage reaction. Here the child is more responsive, can better perceive what is happening outside of herself, and will be more receptive to the parent's efforts at mitigating the experience. When the mother feels the rage reaction is in its down climb, she can then become active: offering to comfort the child, talking to the child about what is going on, and encouraging the child to get a hold of herself. The child may not accept Mother's efforts to help right then, but such efforts are warranted because they eventually do help.

Here we must refer again to our discussion of limit setting. Many distressed children will turn to Mother and plead for comforting through signs of wanting or asking to be held, or by leaning into the mother's body. This is a highly favorable signal for the resolution of the tantrum, and the time is highly favorable for the parent's intervention. We say with a significant degree of urgency that it is important for parents to accept a child's plea for comfort. When, during the down limb of the rage reaction, the infant appeals for comforting, this signals the optimal condition for the parent's intervention and for the possibility of its being effective.

As all mothers know, children will not always appeal for comforting during the down limb of their component-wave rage reactions. Even when the infant does not appeal for comforting, the mother or father should offer it at that moment. As we noted before, an infant may reject the parent's offer of comforting. We encourage parents not to take this rejection too painfully. True, it may be an expression of rage toward the parent. However, we all know the child is angry—most likely *very* angry—with the parent at this time; therefore we should not be surprised at the child's rejecting the parent's offer of comfort.

Let's go back to 13-month-old Mary, that wonderful little girl who was running into difficulties with her beloved mother in the course of limit setting. As Mary illustrates, quite commonly young children have temper tantrums when the mother or father sets limits.

Mary cried angrily, waved her left arm in a striking movement against her mother several times, and kicked at her from a distance. Twice she actually struck her mother with her arm, and once she also struck herself. We felt that 13-month-old Mary was showing significant evidence of distress. For the first time, her mother could not comfort her crying, as she had before. Here is what we recorded:

> Mary is crying angrily in her mother's arms, she seems to want to get out of those arms; her mother puts her down gently, without observable rejection, and Mary cries even more loudly and angrily. Her mother cannot hold and cannot put her down. She does pick her up and continues to hold her while sitting in a chair, and Mary calms down some. As she sits on her mother's lap, she does not lean back into her mother's body—which she has always done easily—but rather sits upright, separated from her mother's torso. Mrs. W., wanting to comfort her more actively, reaches to touch Mary's arm; Mary pushes her hand away, in an unequivocal gesture of rejection. A moment later this is repeated. Mary's affect is sober and serious. . . . [Now] her mother stopped actively trying to comfort her.
>
> After Mary's remaining 30–60 seconds so poised, Mrs. W. got up carrying her daughter and tried to distract her by going to the toy box. Suddenly, as Mrs. W. bent down, Mary began to cry as if she has been struck by a blow. Mother and observers were startled. When her mother returned to her chair, Mary calmed quickly and again sat upright on her mother's lap. Gradually, her body tone softened and she relaxed passively into her mother's body, thumb in mouth, where she remained, awake, for 20–30 minutes. [1979, pp. 204–205]

We read several things into what we saw. Mother's effort to comfort Mary was rejected. Mother was sensitively responsive to Mary's rejection and did not reject her child. After a while of sitting passively with her child on her lap,

Mother made another effort to comfort and perhaps distract Mary from her large internal feeling of distress. But we then saw Mary protest Mother's effort to comfort and distract her. Her reaction led the mother back to where she was before, sitting with Mary on her lap, remaining seemingly passive.

However, Mother's passively holding her infant was a superbly active intervention. She afforded Mary the opportunity to make further efforts to get hold of herself, work through her rage toward her mother, and calm herself down. In a home setting, if a child were to have that kind of reaction, a mother might not find it reasonable to just sit there and hold her enraged and distressed child for a period of 20 or 30 minutes. Nonetheless, we were impressed by the beneficial effect of Mary's being held by her mother and by her mother's emotional and physical availability while Mary was doing the internal work of getting over her rage reaction.

It is sometimes difficult for a mother, who always has too much to do, to recognize the enormous value and benefit of sitting for 20 or 30 minutes with an infant who is overcoming a temper tantrum. But we assert that it is, in fact, timesaving, emotionally protective, well-being securing, and more, for a mother to spend that kind of time in that kind of effort under conditions of a tantrum experience.

It is in this context, during the down limb of a component-wave rage reaction, that a parent's interventions will be received by the child in a constructive, tantrum resolving way. Mother or Father should repeat limit setting admonitions, if the tantrum emerged in the course of limit setting.

Repeating an admonition in the course of comforting can be helped by an empathic comment, such as "It is hard to not be able to have what we want. But I am sorry, you cannot have Tommy's truck. It belongs to him." And if the child allows you to get that far, at an opportune moment you might also want to add something like, "I wouldn't let Tommy take what belongs to you, and I can't let you take what belongs to Tommy."

Nor should the parent give up when her effort to comfort is rejected. The fact that the infant is rejecting the mother's comforting or the mother's now-benevolent admonition should not be taken as a sign that the mother's effort is not working. We all know the positive impact such a gesture has on us when we are angry with someone. Before we are ready to respond in a conciliatory way, we may well be aware of the other person's efforts to be conciliatory. Most often such efforts are appreciated by us, even if we are not yet ready to reciprocate in kind. So, too, the infant hears the mother's efforts, and even if she is not ready to reciprocate in kind, is soothed and comforted by them.

Let us add a few notes to dealing with a tantrum. It is helpful if a parent can not get *too* angry with the child having a tantrum. Knowing that the child may be traumatized by acute pain and excessive unpleasure, feels terribly helpless, ineffectual, and often threatened and disorganized, can help a parent not become too angry with the child.

When between outbursts of rage—between component-wave rage reactions—the child wants to be held, by all means do so. However, the child may not want to be held, even then. Offer to do so, but don't force yourself on the child. Do try to calm her with soothing comments. "Come on, Sweetie, get hold of yourself. Calm down." This may not work immediately and should be repeated several times.

If the tantrum arises in a context of setting limits, it is best not to blame the tantrum on something else. Acknowledge to the child that you are aware that by setting limits, you are perhaps causing the child to have the tantrum. Nonetheless, when you find that the limit is needed, you have to persist. The parent's avoiding the awareness that she or he instigated the tantrum through setting limits will only make it more difficult for the child to resolve the rage reaction.

If the tantrum is caused by a limit that the parent sets and subsequently sees is not really needed—and we reiterate that limits should be set only when they are truly needed—the parent should have the courage and good sense to back off. Tell your child you have thought things over and have changed your mind. But tell her that you changed your mind not because she had a blooming fit, but because you feel your limit is not needed, as you originally felt it was.

We have said that putting the child in a room by herself when she is having a tantrum may be harmful. The threat of being abandoned is then superimposed on the trauma of the tantrum. To be abandoned at that time is to be abandoned when one is flat on one's back.

However, there is a time when such a separation may be warranted: when the parent fears losing control of herself and physically abusing the child. We recommend that the parent then tell the child why she is leaving. When the child is sent to her room, the child is most likely to feel it is because she is unbearable. It is important to be brave and honest with the child and tell her that the reason Mother is putting her in her room is because she fears losing control herself. "You're driving me up a wall, and I can't help you right now. In fact, I am afraid I am going to hurt you. For that reason, I am going to go to my room for a while. You go to your room for a while, too." You should let a child know when she is driving you up a wall, even if it upsets her—which it will—or even if she may not be able to hear what you are saying.

Under these conditions, it is imperative that the parent talk to the child after the tantrum has subsided. She should say she regrets having had to put the child in her room, and the reason she did so is that she was so upset by what was going on that she feared she might do something she would later feel very bad about. We would furthermore add that a parent could then make it a task for the child and for herself to make every effort to try to control herself when feeling so angry. All parents get angry, because we all suffer experiences that produce excessive unpleasure in us. As parents, we need to learn to develop sufficient controls over our hostility when it is mobilized.

We would conclude this section on dealing with temper tantrums and rage reactions by recommending that, after the tantrum has subsided, parents talk with their children about the events that led to the tantrum and about the necessity for learning to deal better with them. A review of the events that have caused tantrums and may recur can help lessen the stress they may bring and help prevent their repetition. Here, of course, we advocate a comforting, respectful dialogue, rather than a moralistic or punitive one.

CHAPTER 8

Helping the Child Cope with Painful Emotional Feelings

Coping with Anxiety

Mrs. J. was puzzled. She is a very perceptive and tuned-in mother. She had told her 3-year-old son, Kenny, that she would be out shopping while he was taking his nap, that Grandma was there, and that she'd be back soon. When she came back, Kenny was at the window and, on seeing her, gave her a beaming smile. He seemed clearly happy to see her. But when she walked into the house carrying bags, he was scowling and outrightly angry with her! Okay, he was mad at her being out, but she had told him she would be!

We told her it had been very helpful that she told him. But, even though she prepared him for it, such preparation did not prevent his experiencing separation anxiety of sufficient intensity that it generated hostility in him. On seeing her, he was greatly relieved and happy. And then, secure that Mother had come home, the anger the anxiety had generated came to the surface. Because he felt safe enough with Mother, he could let her know just exactly how he was feeling!

Bearing in mind the critical formula that excessive unpleasure generates hostility, we want to help parents be aware of the fact that, from the first months of life, human beings are capable of experiencing feelings that bring them a great deal of emotional pain. Certainly by the middle of the first year of life, children are capable of experiencing anxiety, as well as feeling painfully ungratified and abandoned.

Because such emotional reactions can be very painful, we want to help parents intervene in ways that can mitigate such experiences and thereby generate and mobilize less hostility. We want to help parents try to prevent undue anxiety, enable them to help the child cope constructively with current anxiety, and teach them to help the child work through anxiety reactions that occur.

Similarly, we will do the same for feelings of depression. Although there are other emotional reactions that create pain—envy, jealousy, fear, and shame—we shall not deal directly with them. It is our hope that helping parents understand and deal with anxiety and depression will enable them to figure out ways of dealing constructively with other painful emotional reactions.

Anxiety is the child's feeling helpless in the face of what he experiences as danger. When it is intense, since it is very painful, anxiety generates hostility. It is important for parents to know what anxiety looks like, sounds like, and feels like in their child. Also it is useful to know what kinds of experiences commonly cause anxiety in children.

Under 5 years of age, the most common sources of anxiety are: separations from parents; strangers; the fear of losing the love of one's parents; the fear of bodily harm; the dread of losing one's autonomy and sense of self. We will also talk briefly about sources of anxiety in children older than 5 and in adolescents. All these experiences create a situation in which the child or adolescent feels helpless and vulnerable. Therefore, it helps for the child to know that he is not alone in attempting to deal with what is causing the helplessness. Make efforts to comfort and calm your child (or adolescent) before, during, and after anxiety reactions. This includes talking about and dealing with both the child's (or adolescent's) anxiety and the hostility that his anxiety generated or mobilized.

While anxiety is the feeling of helplessness in the face of an inner, undefined danger, depression is the reaction experienced after that event has occurred. The threat of danger has materialized, and now there are feelings of helplessness, hopelessness, and of giving up. Since depression is painful, when it is intense, it, too, generates hostility. This is especially evident in that when children recover from depression, one of the first signs of recovery may be that they become angry, or even overtly hostile and destructive.

It is important to know what depression looks like in your child or adolescent and to acknowledge it when it is there. Next it helps to try to figure out what could be causing the child's or adolescent's feelings of depression. The loss of a loved one, a severe disappointment, persisting deprivation of basic needs, or the child's or teenager's feeling that he is bad or doing unacceptable things, are common sources of depressive feelings. If at all possible, it helps to undo the source of the depression. Where circumstances causing a depression cannot be undone, make efforts to comfort and be available to your child or teenager. This includes empathic nurturing where indicated, as well as talking about and dealing with both the child's or adolescent's depression and the hostility this depression has generated or mobilized.

Overall, we want to help parents develop an emotional dialogue with their children about all painful feelings. First, we shall talk about dealing with anxiety, and then about dealing with depression.

Rationale

Anxiety—the child's feeling helpless in the face of what he experiences as a danger—is a common experience. It clearly becomes evident from about the middle of the first year of life on, although some children as young as 4 months show evidence of it. Anxiety needs to be dealt with constructively, especially when it occurs in its extreme form, which we know as panic reactions. Anxiety is very painful and therefore is a generator of hostility. This hostility may not become manifest in behavior. It may be turned against the self or appear in the form of irritability and moodiness. It may also be expressed directly. In its extreme form, as panic reactions, anxiety is sure to cause hostility. Even when the anxiety has abated, it may produce an after reaction of anger—and even rage—that will dissipate if worked through. When anxiety is not worked through, it is likely that the generated hostility will not dissipate well.

Interventional Steps

First, it is important for parents to try to identify what anxiety looks like, sounds like, and feels like in their child. If they can do so with their young child, they will be able to do so when that child becomes an adolescent. To be able to recognize anxiety in one's child, the parent will have to empathize with what the child is feeling. With anxiety, depression, and all painful feelings, trying to perceive and empathize with what the child is feeling is of primary importance.

In the mental-health field, anxiety is said to be "a feeling of impending doom." It is likely that most parents would readily identify anxiety in its extreme form—a panic state. To identify what a panic state looks like, simply imagine that you were feeling panicky. What do you feel like? What do you look like? What sound do you make? Similar sounds and appearance will be evident in the child.

For milder states of anxiety, the infant may look apprehensive, frightened, or bewildered. Age will influence the sounds the child may make. For example, the older child may verbalize fear and apprehension. Prior to language capability, the parent will have to rely on preverbal sounds such as crying, whimpering, and exclamations of apprehension and fear. In terms of bodily communication, very commonly a young child (from 4 months of age on) will cling when near the parent – and cling with a pressure that may feel quite uncomfortable to the parent.

Remember the two principal ways in which one's empathy can be sharpened. The first is to listen to the child, look at the child, feel what the child may be feeling. Ask yourself how you would be feeling if you looked as the child does, sounded and felt like the child seems to feel. In other words, put yourself in your child's shoes and ask yourself what that would feel like to you.

The second way is the converse. Start by asking yourself what you would look like, sound like, and feel like if you were experiencing helplessness in the face of a danger, or how you would feel if you were in a panic state. Then check to see if that is how your child appears to you. Whichever way works best for you, use it.

It is impossible to totally prevent the occurrence of anxiety. In fact, it may not even be desirable to do so, if one could. Be that as it may, it is not possible to prevent anxiety totally, whatever the parents' efforts. However, once you recognize anxiety in your child, you should attempt to prevent its gathering momentum, increasing in intensity, being repeated frequently, and going unaddressed. In order to prevent undue anxiety, it is useful to know what kinds of experiences commonly cause anxiety in the early years.

Mental health professionals have proposed that anxiety reactions are normal at given developmental periods. These reactions have been organized by psychoanalytic researchers–clinicians as consisting of a series of emotionally perceived dangers that emerge sequentially during the course of normal development. Let us underscore that these are *normal* reactions.

The best-delineated series of anxiety reactions that normally occurs in children starts with separation anxiety and stranger anxiety. These become manifest at about 5 to 6 months of age and last for several years. To a degree, these last in human beings indefinitely. These anxieties occur for the following reason: The 5- to 6-month-old, having established an emotional attachment to the mother, now experiences separation anxiety when Mother leaves. This is because at that age, the infant cannot yet retain the image of the mother in mind when she is not present; thus, the child feels as if Mother has disappeared.

The second common source of anxiety is the fear of losing the love of one's parents. This anxiety tends especially to occur from the end of the first year of life through the second year. This anxiety also tends to remain with human beings to some degree, for an indefinite period of time.

The third major source of anxiety is that associated with fear of bodily harm and fear of losing vital body parts, especially the genitals. This fear may emerge in the latter half of the second year, in some children. It usually occurs at about $2^1/2$ years of age and runs an acute course through the fifth or sixth year of life, after which it may subside. Again, like the other sources of anxiety, it may remain with an individual, to a more or less intense degree, for a longer or shorter period of time.

These major sources of anxiety are commonly evident in the behavior of children under 5 years. For instance, 2½-year-old Robbie's pants were not zippered. Mother, seeing this fact, called him to her and quite casually and gently began to reach for the zipper and pull it up. Robbie sharply pulled away from his mother, with a look of distress on his face. It is not uncommon for boys of this age to show evidence of acute anxiety in the face of what they misconstrue to be a danger to their penis. Similarly, a younger child, say a 16-month-old, may cry, reach out for, and cling to Mother when she is about to leave for work. The distress is clearly tied up with separation from the mother and the anxiety that stirs up.

From about 2 to 3 years of age, the source of anxiety may be difficult to discern from the child's behavior and may even be unknown to the child. For instance, a 3-year-old who has trouble going to bed may be afraid of the dark and/or of going to sleep. It may not be clear whether the child is coping with feelings of separation, feelings of being unloved by Mother, or feelings of being punished for having hostile feelings or transgressive thoughts. The 4-year-old's fear that a big black bear is going to come and get him most likely pertains to some oedipal conflict and rivalry with his father, or with castration anxiety. However, the child will not be aware of its source.

Other distressing behaviors—such as phobias, nightmares, sleep difficulties—all bring with them a significant degree of anxiety, without clearly revealing what the underlying sources might be.

In addition to anxiety arising out of some undetermined

inner conflict, young children also often react to some stimuli with sharp fear. This often looks like anxiety and causes a great deal of pain and excessive unpleasure. For instance, 2- and 3-year-olds are known to experience reactions of fear and distress from loud noises, sirens, barking dogs, motorcycles, and fights between parents. These fear reactions can be significantly helped by the way parents deal with them.

All of these experiences bring with them excessive unpleasure and therefore have the potential for generating or mobilizing hostility in the child. Although the hostility may not immediately become evident, we assume that if the experience is sufficiently pain producing, it will generate hostility in the child, even if that hostility does not become manifest in behavior or is not discharged right away.

All of these experiences create a situation in which the child feels more or less helpless and vulnerable. Therefore, one critical way of helping a child is to help him feel he is not alone in attempting to deal with what is causing the helplessness. Again, this is an instance where a parent can act in the child's behalf as a helping hand. It is very helpful when the child feels the parent is making an effort to help him cope with the danger and anxiety.

For instance, a 4-year-old boy is awakened from a frightening dream in which a big bear is chasing him. Mother or Father may not understand what the dream is about—and if she or he does, interpretation by parents is replete with hazards and great care has to be exercised. But even without addressing the meaning of the dream, the child may be comforted by the parent's gently saying, "That was a scary dream. You're having some scary thoughts. Mommy and I are here to help, anytime. And, there are no bears here. . . . " Side by side with this reassurance, the parent's comforting helps to decrease the child's anxiety.

It is important for parents to learn to distinguish anxiety and fear from orneriness, which is well described by the phrase, "I want what I want when I want it!" Both require a response from the parent. However, the responses should be different. Anxiety-induced or fear-induced crying requires talking about what is upsetting the child, reassurance, and comforting. Orneriness requires empathic and reasonable limit setting.

But how can you tell whether the child is experiencing anxiety or being ornery? The parent must rely on his empathic resonating with the child's experiencing. As we have said before, put yourself in the child's position. If you were behaving that way, how would you feel? Would you be feeling frightened and helpless? Or are you feeling like the princess who can't get what she wants?

It is important that parents trust their readings of their children's emotional reactions and the feelings that their children arouse within them.

Much of our discussion in this book is directed to the parents of children under 6 years of age. However, much of it also applies to parenting elementary-school-age children and adolescents, although age-appropriate modifications are required. So, let us continue the series of anxiety sources through these years, as well.

The fourth major source of anxiety is intimately linked with the fear of losing the parent's love: the fear of disapproval by our own consciences. During the fourth to sixth years, the child's conscience develops to the degree that he is now governed by it. At that point, transgressive wishes and acts lead to strong feelings of guilt. Guilt is the disapproval of our own conscience. We all know how much we want to avoid feelings of guilt. During the period from about 5 to 10 years of age, the threat of disapproval by our recently developed and consolidating conscience is an uppermost source of anxiety.

The fifth major source of anxiety emerges during puberty: the fear of being governed by the powerful pressure of our sexuality. Side by side with this is anxiety produced by the enlarging body and the much more powerful capability to act on one's aggression. When a father is overly hostile to his 15-year-old son, that son perceives his wish to react with equal hostility toward his father as highly threatening, because of his increasingly more powerful body. The fantasy of killing his father may become alarming; it is a major source of anxiety during adolescence.

There are other sources of anxiety that occur in the course of development – the dread of losing one's autonomy and sense of self, or the adolescent's dread of disapproval by his peers. Each requires parental patience and efforts to understand them. Anxiety is painful, and although it is often not resolvable by parents, they can lessen its impact on the child by the way they help the child deal with it.

Dealing with an Anxiety Reaction

Let's talk about dealing with an anxiety reaction. Assume that you have a 9-month-old child and are about to leave for work or for an appointment. Your child is crying, tremulous, in despair, and may be clinging to you. You know this reaction is produced by the fact that you are about to leave. You are now feeling very upset, even to the point of canceling your appointment or not going to work because of the guilt you are feeling and because you are being torn apart by your infant's reaction.

If it is necessary for you to go, then tell your child that. Yes, you speak to a 9-month-old. You tell a 9-month-old where you have to go and why you have to go. You tell your child that you will be back, and when—using indicators that a child may understand. "Before you go to sleep, Mommy will be back," or "Before we eat again, Mommy will be back."

You also tell the child that the substitute caregiver will take good care of him while you are away, and that you are ready to leave. Efforts to comfort while you are talking are useful, although they may not be as effective as you would like. In fact, it is likely that your child may not calm down before you go, and you may feel all your efforts are for nought.

Years of work with mothers and their infants make it quite clear to us that even though a parent's efforts to comfort the child and calm the child's anxiety may not bring immediate results, in the long run, such efforts do build a base of security, trust, and feeling cared for within the child. This trust decreases the level of anxiety and unpleasure experienced at times of separation and leads to a lessening of the generation of hostility.

There are going to be times when your child experiences

anxiety that you cannot alleviate. Efforts to alleviate that anxiety ought to be made anyway, because they ultimately bring results, even if they do not undo the underlying source or totally alleviate the immediate experience of distress. The best that can be aimed for in helping a child who is anxious is to convey the sense that you want to help and to try and lessen that feeling of anxiety as best you can.

The second step in working on relieving, stopping, or alleviating anxiety is to work through the anxiety reaction when it is in the process of waning or has stopped. For instance, coming back to the mother who has to go to work, which requires her leaving her 16-month-old boy.

> You have left your infant crying. You were distressed and feeling terribly guilty. All in all, it was a very difficult episode. Now you are coming back home, and you are not quite comfortable about encountering your child. You walk in the house, and immediately on seeing you, he reacts with a big smile and eagerly extends his arms toward you. Greatly relieved, you rush to your baby, pick him up, and give him a big hug. A moment later, the child hits you. Or, he begins to fuss and, in one way or another, to aggravate you.

We infer the following, which commonly happens: The child is greatly relieved to see you, blissfully happy at the sight of you. But then the memory of his recent pain comes to the foreground, and he is angry with you. Although you are probably tired, you now have the task of facing an angry 16-month-old. Yes, the rascal is angry with you. That's all you needed!

The fact is, your infant's welcoming reaction—both the manifest love feelings and the angry feelings—are the product of the infant's valuing you. The separation anxiety was highly painful to the child, and it produced excessive unpleasure and generated hostility. Since you were the instigator of that pain, that hostility is directed toward you.

Rather than a most unfortunate added burden to your day, we feel this unpleasant encounter is an enormous opportunity in a number of important ways. First of all, it is an opportunity to help the child learn about the realities of life. Second, it is an opportunity to help him learn about human relationships, namely, that people who love each other can get angry with each other without undermining the love in the relationship. In addition, this is an opportunity to talk to the child about: what upset him; why you had to behave as you did; your understanding of how he feels; your feeling upset by the fact that he felt so hurt; that although you can understand his being angry with you, that does not mean you will allow him to hit you, and so forth. It is an opportunity to talk about what caused the child to be upset and angry, in the context of which the parent can be reassuring and comforting. This is an opportunity to repair the hurt caused by the anxiety and undo the hostility it generated.

We want to stress the importance of allowing the child to complain. Allowing the older child to go over the experience and talk it through lessens that experience's traumatizing potential. It is also important to allow the child to express feelings of anger in ways that are acceptable to you.

Not allowing a child's expression of feelings of anger prevents him from working through those feelings of hostility and burdens him with a larger load of hostile feelings. Of course, episodes of this kind may also require your setting limits to help your child learn how to express and discharge hostile feelings in reasonable and acceptable ways.

Coping with Depression

We first saw Richie when he was 14 months old. He looked about 8 months old. His face looked awfully sad and pained, his eyes were dull, and he seemed to look through me. He was subdued, sitting on the floor where his foster mother had put him near her, even though there were other children milling around and toys scattered on the floor. He looked wary of us.

We learned that prior to 6 months of age, he had been cheerful, even charming, gratifyingly interactive, and developing very well physically and emotionally. A serious family problem developed: His young mother and he were abandoned. Mother became very upset, withdrew emotionally from him, and Richie was abused physically. He was placed in a shelter for about seven months, and then he was taken into foster care.

Now, here is the point we want to make. When Richie began to recover and became less depressed, he became physically explosive and destructive. He would throw toys in a seemingly disorganized way, as if unaware that a thrown toy could hurt someone or break something. He would have sharp tantrums at even very slight frustrations, as in play with a lovely 3-year-old girl who seemed to be trying to make him feel better. When young children recover from depression, one of the first signs of recovery may be that they become angry, perhaps even overtly hostile and destructive.

Our aim here is to help parents prevent undue depressions, help parents help their children cope with unavoidable depressions, and help parents help their children work through experiences of depression after they have occurred.

Rationale

Depressions have several contributing sources. Some human beings are endowed with genetic factors that predispose them to react with depression more readily than others. Certain specific types of depression bring inordinate pain and produce significant problems. Whether or not one is born with a genetic predisposition to certain types of depression, human experience brings traumas to our lives that produce depression in all of us. Mental health professionals believe it is essential that human beings all learn to cope with feelings of anxiety and depression. Depression is unavoidable, although, both predispositions and life experiences influence the intensity, frequency, and duration of one's depressions.

Anxiety is the feeling of helplessness in the face of an inner, undefined danger; a feeling of impending doom. Some mental-health clinicians describe depression as the reaction after that event has occurred. For instance, the 16-month-old experiences separation anxiety, which is a feeling of helplessness in anticipation of the mother not being there. Depression is the reaction of loss he feels when, after a period of time, Mother does not return. The threat of danger has materialized, and there are feelings not only of helplessness but of hopelessness and of giving up.

It is imperative that parents know children are capable of suffering from depressive feelings from even the early months of life. By 6 to 8 months, infants are capable of intense feelings that look like sadness, and within months are capable of full-blown serious depressive reactions. Whatever the genetic predisposition in any given child, excessive feelings of deprivation, excessive feelings of rejection, and insufficient attention all tend to lead to depression in an infant, child, or adult. Once a child becomes sufficiently attached to his mother and father—usually by 5 to 6 months of age—the loss of that parent, unless satisfactorily substituted for, will lead to depression. Where a child is insufficiently attached to his parent at 6 months, such a depressive reaction will not occur. But this is no consolation, because a 5- to 6-month-old's not having formed a specific attachment to his mother brings effects that may be more dire than depression. The point we want to emphasize here is that infants become capable of experiencing depressive feelings from the middle of the first year of life. Prior to that age, excessive deprivations and insufficient attachments usually do not lead to depressive feelings, but will lead to withdrawal and even failure to grow and thrive.

Depression can be exceedingly painful. Its consequences

for the present (i.e., when it emerges) and for personality formation and development are such that efforts to deal with it are warranted. We underscore that mental-health professionals have long linked depression with the play of excessive feelings of hostility that are directed away from others onto the self, whether the depression is based in guilt, shame, or in reaction to the loss of a loved one.

What we want to emphasize here, is that in addition to the fact that hate and hostility turned against the self lead to depression, insofar as depression is significantly painful, it will usually produce hostility. It will not do so when the hate turned against the self results from guilt, in which case the self-hate is experienced as punishment and will alleviate the guilt. The pain of depression will then be welcomed and may not further mobilize hostility. But not all depression arises from guilt. And it is especially where the pain of depression further mobilizes hostility, that parents can intervene to help their infants and children in a productive way.

A further note of clarification. Clinically, the resolution of depression always shows an associated discharge of what seems to be depression-bound hostility. In fact, the opportunity to express and discharge that hostility in ways tolerable to the self is assumed to be essential for recovery from depression in children, as well as in adults. How that depression-bound hostility is permitted expression and how it is discharged are important to the success of working through the depression. For instance, we know that children recovering from depression will commonly become hostile and difficult to handle, which may cause caregivers to reject them and not allow the needed expression of pent-up rage and hate. This in turn may interfere with their recovery from depression.

Interventional Steps

What does depression look like in children? The principal features of depression or depressive feelings are the same in children (even very young children) as they are in adults. Consider feeling hopeless. What would that look like? Consider that a very painful and traumatizing event has occurred to you. It does not have to be as traumatic as what happened to Richie. Let yourself feel you have just lost someone you value greatly, or that you are severely disappointed in an expectation and there is no hope that the expectation will ever be fulfilled. That is depression.

The infant will look sad, and his facial expression will be flat. When you let yourself feel what the infant's face elicits in you, you will feel sad and hopeless. Like Richie, children who are depressed (even infants as young as 8 or 9 months of age) will tend to withdraw, be inactive, move slowly, and respond to another person's approach with little experience of pleasure. Some infants will even go to sleep.

Depressed children, even infants who crawl or walk will tend to move slowly and sluggishly. Richie, at 14 months, just sat where he was put when we first saw him. The child may refuse to eat, may tend not to demand food and perhaps not even feel hungry, and will respond to efforts to feed him with sluggishness. A 3-year-old or a 7-year-old experiencing these feelings is not at all difficult to identify.

Sadness hurts, and when it hurts enough it generates hostility.

We learned a number of years ago, especially in studying a 3-year-old whose father died, that adults have much difficulty in seeing the various expressions of pain that children show. From this 3-year-old and other children, we learned that a major obstacle to an adult's recognizing depression in children comes from the adult's denying the child's painful feelings. It is just too difficult for many of us to acknowledge that children can suffer so. This fact makes it difficult for adults to help depressed children.

An added note may be warranted: It is not only parents who have difficulty recognizing when a young child is depressed. For example, a number of years ago, in preparation for a professional presentation and discussion, several child psychiatrists reviewed a video presentation prepared by one of our well-regarded colleagues, the aim of which was to illustrate how difficult it is for children to acknowledge and deal with the death of a parent. The tape showed a 3-year-old's nursery-school activities soon following the death of her mother by cancer. In several close reviews of this tape, we found five instances in which the child made reference to hospitals, illness, as well as her mother, each of which was stifled by the well-meaning nursery-school teacher. They were not talking about that at the time, the child was told. What we infer to be the child's efforts to talk about her mother's illness, hospitalizations, and eventual death were obstructed. This occurred in a nursery that was part of a psychiatric clinic and research center. Our intention is not to criticize. It is, rather, to point out what we learned from it: Helping a depressed child deal with his feelings, thoughts, and fantasies is extremely difficult for adults, even for teachers and possibly for some psychotherapists. It is quite clear that without opening oneself to experiencing a young child's depression, one cannot hope to help the child cope with it constructively.

The first step then is to know what depression looks like and to acknowledge it when it is there!

Dealing with a Reaction of Depression

The next step is to try to sort out what could be causing the child's feeling of depression. The loss of a loved one, a severe disappointment, a persisting deprivation of basic needs—attention, cuddling, a show of love, or the child's own feeling that he is bad—all of these may precipitate depressive feelings. In a 3- or 4-year-old, a move, the loss of a dear little friend, the loss of a favorite caregiver (other than a parent) can also produce feelings of depression.

When one knows the source of the depression, if it can be undone, it is wise to do so. For instance, if an infant is showing signs of sadness because Mother has been in the hospital two days for surgery, it would be helpful to telephone the mother and have the infant hear her voice. Better still, if you can work it out with your doctor and the hospital—and we encourage parents to make such demands—take the infant to see the mother in the hospital. An infant who shows feelings of sadness because Mother has gone to the hospital will most likely recover from those feelings when the mother returns home—if the separation has not been too long, say a few days, and the child is helped to work through the depressive reaction based on his feeling of loss.

Some parents are afraid to call, because the child will be upset on hearing Mother's voice. True, the child will be upset. But the fact is that the child already is upset, whether he shows it or not. In fact, the longer the absence and the silence, the more intense and entrenched the upset feelings become. The less the distress is vocalized, the more it becomes embedded in the psyche. Therefore, although unpleasant, it is better to call than not call.

Young infants who are left with caregivers when parents go on a one- or two-week vacation, or on a six-week work assignment, may react with feelings of depression that need to be dealt with by telephone calls or a prompt return (when possible) home.

Where circumstances that cause depression cannot be undone, compensatory action against the source of the depression can be instituted, for example, talking about Mother's being in the hospital, explanations as to why she had to go there, reassurance as to when she will come back. These are basic requisites to help the child cope with depressive feelings — even infants under 1 year of age. Comforting in the face of painful feelings is always a worthwhile effort. Empathic nurturing is always helpful in the face of depression, even when the reaction to that empathic nurturing and comforting does not seem to work right away.

Since one of the common causes of depression in early childhood is due to a feeling of having lost Mother's love, such as following disruptive behavior, talking about what caused the mother's anger and reassuring that the loss of that love is temporary, if indeed present at all, will be very helpful.

Most important in helping a child overcome feelings of depression is the necessity to allow the child to express and discharge feelings of hostility that are bound to the depression and mobilized by it. The parent has to allow, tolerate, and help the child find acceptable ways of expressing hostility. Allowing the child to complain, to fuss, to cry, to verbalize ("Bad Mommy!") is essential.

Again, explaining why the depression-inducing event occurred is important: "Now Mommy is well and doesn't have to go to the hospital anymore," or, "Mommy needs to go to work." It is essential for the parent to allow the child to react to explanations.

Such complaining and explanations always need more than one go-round. Each such complaint and explanation contributes to the working through and the lessening of the traumatizing effects of the event that caused the depression.

The earlier such dialogues occur, the better. Again, we want to emphasize that talking to an infant who cannot yet talk is most appropriate, feasible, and helpful. Telling a 10-month-old "I am sorry I upset you," or "I'm sorry that what I did hurt you," has beneficial effects. First, the child will feel your empathy, which is critical for many reasons. Second, the child will feel that what he is experiencing is appropriate, permissible, unavoidable, and understood, and efforts are being made to make the painful feelings go away.

Helping the child find ways to express and discharge the depression-bound hostility in ways that are acceptable to both the child and the parents is a vital task.

CHAPTER 9

Optimizing the Parent–Child Relationship

We have now addressed six types of parent–child interactions where aggression—in both its nondestructive and its hostile, destructive form—is commonly at play and can be lessened or intensified. We have found that in these interactions, parents have opportunities to substantially help their children. Our discussions of these interactions can inform parents on ways to deal with other interactions we did not talk about.

In this chapter, we want to talk about what we believe to be the most important single goal parents ought to aim for in their efforts to help their children grow emotionally healthy: to optimize their relationships with their children.

Optimizing your relationship with your child does not mean always being lovingly reassuring, praising, pleasant, and nice. There are times to be annoyed and angry, to be troubled and worried, to register disapproval and scold. It is complex. Whatever your child's inborn dispositions, strengths, and vulnerabilities, the relationship you have with your child is the most powerful vehicle you have for mediating and influencing her emotional development and her emotional life.

Our aim is to enhance and optimize the parent–child relationship throughout its course, from infancy through adolescence. We hope to help parents promote the development of a positive attachment with their children, because a sufficiently positive relationship between parent and child is of enormous importance to the healthy development of aggression in the child.

A sufficiently positive emotional attachment helps promote development in general and enhances the development of autonomy and assertiveness. It counters the development of excessive hostility in a number of ways. First, forming a positive attachment requires that, to a reasonable degree, the parent respond helpfully to the child's basic emotional needs. Rejection, inadequate fulfillment of the child's basic emotional needs, and too much frustration have to be significantly outweighed by gratifications. This means that less hostility is mobilized in the child, which secures identification with the parents in a prevailingly positive mode. This will enhance love-based compliance rather than fear-based compliance and rejection of the parents' efforts to socialize the child.

In forming a positive relationship between parent and child, the parent is loading the love side of the inevitable ambivalence that occurs in every parent–child relationship. This love loading helps to outweigh the child's feelings of hate for the parent. Loading the positive side of the child's ambivalence gives a better balance of love and hostility and better motivates the development of controls.

Also, it helps secure healthier conscience formation and will protect against the development of highly troublesome and unhealthy patterns of adaptation.

Finally, a positive parent–child relationship is the most powerful tool parents have for working through and lessening the inevitable hate and hostility the child experiences. This protects against large accumulations of hostility in the child. Therefore, whatever the child's psychological-emotional endowment, through protecting against large generations and accumulations of hostility, a sufficiently positive parent–child relationship protects against the development of excessive hostility in the child.

Over the course of a child's life, each stage of development brings with it specific challenges. Helping a child master these developmental challenges promotes a positive attachment between parent and child. From the other side, those factors that enhance attachment are also the ones that promote the child's healthy development of autonomy, assertiveness, and sense of being a valued, a capable, and an independent self.

In developing a positive parent–child relationship, the primary factor is the parent's loving the child and being with the child in such a way that her love is evident. Hand in hand with this is the parent's helpful responsiveness to the child's communication of needs for positively toned involvement with the parent, for other interactions such as limit setting, and for autonomy. Still another factor is the parent's being able to communicate helpfully with her child, to establish an emotional dialogue with the child. In order to be sufficiently responsive to a child, it helps for a

The emotional dialogue is clear: There is good reciprocity in the mother–child molding and feeling tone. It feels good for both. Such moments optimize their relationship.

parent to understand what the child is experiencing. We feel that if a parent understands developmental issues—

how children develop and communicate—the parent will be better able to be responsive to the child's needs and establish an emotional dialogue with the child. This will enhance the positive attachment between parent and child.

Therefore, the first portion of this chapter will be organized around a discussion of developmental phases and tasks: attachment, the development of autonomy and sense of self, and infantile sexuality. Then we will briefly consider issues of school-age children and adolescents. In the next section, we will discuss some further thoughts on optimizing the parent–child relationship. In this we will focus on general characteristics of growth-promoting relationships, how children (and adults) develop, and how children (and adults) communicate emotionally. In the final section, we will focus on ways to promote the positive attachment between parent and child. Throughout all of these sections, we will consider typical problems that arise and helpful parental interventions.

What We Know about Human Attachment

Infants are born with the disposition, basic mechanisms, and an inner pressure to form an emotional relationship with those who invest emotionally in them. Infants tend to seek out the caregiver, turn to, and emotionally attach to that caregiver.

We now know that—by virtue of having been in the mother's uterus and by virtue of the gradual development of sensory systems—the infant is already acquainted with her mother's voice, the quality and degree of activity of the mother, and perhaps more. Recent studies have shown that during the third trimester of pregnancy, the fetus is responsive to certain external stimuli, such as noises, strong lights aimed at the mother's abdomen, and other stimuli. Thus infants, even at this point, are already becoming acquainted with aspects of the outside world. The newborn responds to the sound of the mother's voice, as compared to that of others, and distinguishes the odor of her mother's body and breast pad, as compared to those of another.

Infants are born with ready-to-go systems that secure emotional attachment. These inborn systems make conditioning possible, as well as the patterning of responsiveness, the accumulation of memory, the ability to be attentive to stimuli, and more. Once born, many a newborn will tend to look at the human face more attentively than other features of her environment. For instance, 12-day-old Bernie, in the course of being fed by his mother, interrupts the feeding and looks at his mother's eyes and forehead. His looking at her is not indifferent; it seems as though he is trying to "take in" the image at which he is staring. We infer that the infant is attempting to assimilate the experience he is having, is linking the feeding process and the gratification it brings with the features of the caregiver who is doing the feeding.

The face of the caregiver, particularly the eyes, forehead, and hairline, constitutes a configuration that elicits in the infant a response of attentiveness—a powerful configuration to which the infant will attach. At about 5 to 6 weeks, most infants will begin to respond to that facial configuration with a smiling response that has the distinctive feature of appearing to be a social smiling response. That is, the smile now seems to be clearly in response to the presentation of that facial configuration. Some of us believe this response is inborn and is a cardinal factor in setting in motion the infant's emotional attachment to the caregiver, now at a new level of organization and experience. We owe our largest debt for understanding this, and much of what will follow, to Dr. René Spitz, who did much of his work in the 1940s and 1950s.

Thus, at about 5 to 6 weeks, in conjunction with a number of physiological and psychological maturations, the appearance of the *social smiling response* heralds the beginning of an emotional attachment that is critical for both infant and parent. Who among us can resist responding to the magnificent smile of a 6-week-old infant? It arouses in the parent a feeling of being recognized and identified by one's own child. Most parents react to the infant's smile by a global response of love and reciprocity. This, of course, is only the beginning of an infant's signs of love.

At this age, the infant is not yet capable of love, but this is where it begins. Some mothers are enormously disappointed and distressed when their 3-day-old infants are not smiling in response to their demonstrations of affection. Knowing that an infant is not capable of a social smile until about 5 to 6 weeks—in some infants, even until 3 months— will protect many first-time parents from feeling they have an unresponsive infant. Since early responsiveness between parent and infant plays a crucial part in the attachment process, it is important that young parents not be disheartened or feel rejected by the very young infant's not being capable of this more advanced kind of responsiveness.

Knowing that the social smiling response does not occur until the second month or so of life will also ready the parent and facilitate the response that will complement their infant's earliest social smiles. The parent's response to the infant's social smile is a critical factor in enhancing not only the social smile, but also the feeling of being responded to appropriately and affectionately. This will enlarge the pathways of mutual responsiveness, of what some have called "the emotional dialogue," between parent and infant.

However, the social smiling response of the 6-week-old infant is, in essence, indiscriminate. That is to say, the infant is primed to respond to a configuration of the human face with a social smile. Therefore, the smiling response will initially be elicited by any face, even by a diagram of a face drawn on a piece of paper. Although it is a social reaction directed toward a person, it is indiscriminate. It is, however, likely that an infant will smile more readily and broadly at her own mother, because by 6 weeks, she will respond more selectively to her mother's voice and odor—aspects of her mother she comes to recognize even before she recognizes her face.

One young mother was upset by the fact that her 3-month-old smiled at other people. It was her hope that the infant had already identified her as a specific person, as someone the infant could distinguish from all other people in a stable fashion. Although the infant was able to discriminate her mother from others in particular ways—by her voice and caregiving features—she had not yet developed the capability to discriminate her mother emotionally stably from others.

The process of emotionally discriminating, with more specificity, who Mother is, who Father is, and even who Brother and Sister are, occurs from about the second or third month of life through the fifth, sixth, and seventh month. In other words, from 3 through 5 months of age (in some children, 6 or 7 months of age), the infant more and more recognizes—cognitively and emotionally—the mother as different from others and gradually more stably smiles at her preferentially. The infant's smiling has now become a specific social smiling response. At about 5 to 7 months, the infant has a somewhat stable feeling of who her prime caregivers are and who the persons are who are emotionally attached to her. She seems to sense who emotionally values her. The infant shows evidence of being first attached to the mother, then to the father, then to siblings and the few people who may frequently appear in her life.

Hand in hand with this, the infant will stop smiling at people whom she does not know. The 5- or 6-month-old may even react to people she does not know with an emotional reaction of distress. This stranger response can have a wide range, from sober curiosity in looking at a stranger to acute reactions of distress and stranger anxiety, with turning away from the stranger and clinging to Mother. This stranger responsiveness will reach a first peak at about 5 to 8 months of age, tend to subside from 10 to 14 months of age, and peak again at about 16 through 24 months of age.

The stranger to the infant is not necessarily a stranger to the family. For instance, visiting grandparents whom the infant has not seen for some time may be experienced by a 5- or 6-month-old as a stranger, and may elicit an acute panic reaction in the infant. This invariably causes distress to the parents, as well as to the visiting grandparents, who are strangers only by virtue of the infant's not having seen them for some time. Usually, if the grandparents take their time about imposing themselves on their grandchild, the infant will soon get used to them, sensing in some way that these grandparents are important to her parents, a factor that will facilitate responsiveness and attachment to the grandparents.

Along with the specific social smiling response and the stranger responses, both of which are indicators of the infant's selective attachment to specific persons (usually the parents), comes the reaction of experiencing anxiety and distress on separation from the parents. A separation reaction is well known to all parents of children from the ages of 5 months to 3 and more years. *Separation reactions* and *separation anxiety*—which is simply a more intense response to separation—are significant indicators that emotional attachment to the child's mother and father is taking place.

Many components of personality depend on an emotional attachment to the caregivers: the capacity for adaptation in a social universe; the development of the ability to relate to other people; the development of satisfactory coping mechanisms; the development of conscience; and other governing personality components. Insufficient attachment may be disastrous or, at best, create serious problems. An absence of attachment to human beings can lead to severe emotional disturbance and antisocial adaptation—adaptation in which human beings are not valued and are treated as things.

Since separation reactions will occur whether the attachment to the parents is satisfactory or not, the presence of these reactions only tells us that a meaningful degree of attachment has taken place. However, because of the enormous importance of the infant's emotional attachment to the parent, this by itself is important information.

Another significant indicator of attachment that complements separation anxiety is the reaction children show when they are reunited with the person to whom they are attached. These *reunion reactions* are of two types. One is the simple positive reunion reaction: On seeing the mother return, the infant is very happy, reaches out to her, may cling to her briefly, but all in all, seems cheerful to see she is back. The second type of reaction is the negative reunion reaction: The infant appears to ignore the mother on her return, or is clearly angry with her when she returns like we saw with 3-year-old Kenny (see Chapter 7). Although the expressed feeling is a negative one, this negative reaction indicates that an emotional attachment exists. Therefore, in and of itself, even a negative reunion reaction is a positive indicator of attachment to the parent.

The specific social smiling response, stranger responses, separation reactions, and reunion reactions are all indicators of attachment to specific persons. In addition, they provide opportunities for parents to facilitate attachment by responding helpfully.

First, when an infant smiles magnificently at the parent, and the parent reacts to that smiling response with a reciprocal show of warmth, tenderness, excitement, and pleasure, this enhances the infant's smiling response and her feeling of being responded to, of being cared for, and of attachment to the parent. It would be difficult to overemphasize the importance of the parent's and infant's experience of mutual joy and pleasure at this stage—or at any time. This experience enriches immeasurably the further development of the infant and of the parent–child relationship.

Next, when the infant experiences a stranger response, how the parent deals with that can enhance attachment to the parent. For example, when Grandfather comes in—convinced that he will be received by the infant with open arms—and receives a reaction of distress, fear, and turning away, it is not uncommon for him to react with distress and push himself onto the infant, attempting to brush aside the stranger response to him. If the grandfather forces himself on the baby, this is going to be experienced by the baby as highly unpleasurable, and will generate hostility, which will not help bring the infant closer to the grandfather.

If the parent of the infant can intervene and convey to Grandfather that he needs to take more time in approaching the infant, and if the parent then attempts to comfort her distressed infant, she will be helping the child cope with her stranger response with greater facility. Also, this will help to eventually bring the infant closer to Grandfather, as well as to the helpful parent. In this way, the parent will be facilitating the child's experiencing, decreasing the duration and intensity of excessive unpleasure, and lessening the generation of hostility in the infant.

Third, when the infant experiences a separation reaction, the parent's handling of that can enhance attachment to the parent. The mother who responds to her infant's separation reactions with a feeling of understanding and moderate personal distress, who tries to comfort her infant, who explains why she has to go, where she has to go, and when she will be back, is making efforts to decrease the intensity of distress the infant is experiencing. And she is doing more. Although this will likely not stop the separation reaction, the mother's efforts will have registered with the infant. They will contribute to ameliorating the infant's pain and ill-feeling and will heighten the positive quality of their mutual attachment while decreasing the hostility generated in her child. We want to say again that by showing concern and making efforts to comfort—even where she cannot stop the pain—the mother is enhancing the child's attachment to her. It will not be lost on the child that the mother is trying to make the child feel better.

And also, the way the parent reacts to the infant's reunion reaction can further facilitate the infant's attachment to the parent. The mother who reacts with pleasure, affection, and attentiveness to an infant reacting positively in reunion conveys to the infant a feeling of being emotionally valued and loved. This enhances the infant's positive feelings toward the mother and increases the positive quality of the infant's attachment to her.

Negative reunion reactions pose more problems for the parent. How does it feel when you come home after having been away from the baby, are very excited about seeing your baby, and your baby is angry with you, like 3-year-old Kenny was (Chapter 7)? It hurts. Again, it is important to allow the child to express the feelings of distress she is experiencing. It is helpful to understand the child is angry because she felt acute anxiety at the parent's absence. This is an indication that the child is attached to you and values you. If the parent can understand the child's anger, can allow it to be expressed in acceptable ways and try to soothe the child, that child will come around more quickly. The feelings of anger toward the parent will not be as intense and will not last as long, and the feelings of affection will return sooner and be heightened. All of these bring a more positive feeling tone to the attachment to the parent.

The mother who reacts to her child's angry reception with, "Well, if you don't want to see me, I don't want to see you!" or another rejecting reaction, will lengthen the duration of hostile reactivity and give the attachment a more negative valence. She will be interfering with the development of a positive attachment.

Finally, there are other behaviors that tell us about attachment. For instance, young children tend to follow the caregiver around as the caregiver moves in the child's environment. Children cry and can be relieved by the caregiver's loving attention better than by others. Children cling to a caregiver in the face of anxiety and distress, whereas they will not cling to others. All of these are indicators of attachment, and all give an opportunity for enhancing attachment.

While holding in mind this outline of the development of attachment, of emotionally valuing the parent (or other caregiver), let's look at it from another vantage point. An essential aspect of this view is that patterns of responsiveness between infant and Mother influence the quality of their relationship from its very beginning. The infant is influenced by her environment from birth on. The assumption that infants do not feel, or that infants cannot remember, is no longer warranted. Quite the contrary. Years of research and clinical work by mental health professionals inform us that infants are sensitive to their experiences from very early on and are affected by them. They do remember, even if only with difficulty and even if they can only with uncertainty reconstruct and verbalize what they experienced in very early childhood. It is much safer to assume that how we impact on our children is going to influence them from the first days of life.

Let us underline that we do not mean traumatic events will remain with the child forever. There are many opportunities in the course of growing up for the resolving of traumatic experiences, for their mitigation, and for the repair of harm that some of these traumas may cause. Parents should never despair about trying to undo, repair, and make up for mistakes they feel they made that may have led to traumatic experiencing in their child. We hold this view even for parents whose children are already grown up. (See Daryl Sifford's *Father and Son*[1] for an excellent example of a father working with his grown son to undo the son's traumatic experiencing of his parents' divorce, which created a major disturbance in the son's relationship to his father.)

Patterns of interaction between infant and parent become established over time, but they do start at the beginning. We know that by a few days of age, infants become habituated to being handled in particular ways and being surrounded by specific odors and specific voices. They show evidence of anticipating specific caregiving when they hear, feel, or smell the particular component features of the caregiver. We think the same also happens for the more complex emotional components of the interaction.

Also, however immature the infant's experiencing, we assume the infant has self feelings, perhaps even the beginnings of a sense of self. In addition, the infant has a primitive awareness of the caregiver—not yet clearly defined, by any means—and is reactive to the interactions between that self and the caregiver. The development of oneself as an individual person goes hand in hand with the development of one's own feelings and awareness of other persons as individuals. The sense of self and others begins to be defined in these earliest interactions with the parents.

Furthermore, the quality of our sense of self, the quality of the way we come to view ourselves, goes hand in hand with the qualities we ascribe to persons with whom we interact and to whom we are emotionally attached. The

---

[1]Philadelphia: Bridgebooks, 1982.

degree to which we love and respect others goes hand in hand with our respect and love for ourselves. Equally, the degree to which we hate and despise others parallels our hating and despising ourselves. In addition, the way others love and respect us makes a large contribution to our loving and respecting ourselves, as the experience of being hated by those we depend on and need contributes to hating and despising ourselves.

The development of the individual is inextricably intertwined with the development of our relationships to others. Where this does not occur, where the development of self is separated from that of our appreciation and valuation of others, conditions of disturbance prevail. This brings significant emotional disturbance and/or antisocial behavior in the self.

In primary relationships, when we experience as unacceptable the hate we feel toward the other person (mother, father, mate, etc.)—a common phenomenon where sufficiently positive relatedness exists—we employ a number of defense mechanisms to make us blind to this hate: denial of hating someone we love; avoiding the awareness of being enraged with someone we love; projecting (ascribing to someone else what one is feeling) the hate we sometimes feel toward our mothers and fathers. All are significant mechanisms we use to protect ourselves against this conflict-producing hate. Another common defense mechanism is that of displacing one's hate and rage toward one's parents onto others, which leads to bullying, scapegoating, and prejudice.

Assuming that the development of a sense of self, the

development of an awareness of the caregiver, and the development of interactive processes begin from the first days of life, we can put these in the context of the model of development conceptualized by Dr. Margaret Mahler. This we call the *separation–individuation* theory.

Separation–Individuation: Becoming a Self Related to Others

Updating slightly the developmental model of separation–individuation, in the earliest weeks of life, the infant experiences the mother as part and parcel of her own universe, as part of the universe that is herself. This includes that which gratifies the infant's demands and needs and quiets the internal pressures which she experiences. However, this is not to be taken to mean that the infant has a clear awareness of and clearly distinguishes all these phenomena. At its peak, the infant begins a process of differentiating out of the child–mother symbiosis. Separation–individuation is Mahler's label for this process. The period during which this differentiation and unfolding occurs is the separation–individuation phase.

At about 6 weeks, the infant begins to have increased awareness of her emerging sense of self and of the configurations and more specific functions of the caregiver. At this time, the infant seems to experience self and Mother as if in a relationship surrounded by an enveloping emotional membrane tying the infant with the caregiver. This emotional oneness forms, during major periods of the infant's waking life, a unitary experience of self–other. A major assumption of one school of psychoanalysis, self psychology, is that our experience of ourselves in relationships to others is as unified, namely as "selfobjects." This holds especially true for this phase of development.

The phase of self–other development we are addressing now, which begins at about 6 weeks of age, was called by Mahler the "normal symbiotic phase." She used this phrase because she wanted to describe her inference, arising from years of work, that the infant experiences the mother as a part of the self and the self as part of the mother, especially during experiences of need and being cared for. It peaks at about 5 to 6 months of age, and then wanes into the other phases of the development of relatedness we are talking about. During this phase, the infant predominantly experiences herself as part and parcel of the caregiver and the caregiver as part of herself, for example, when nursing. There are times when the infant experiences and perceives herself as not attached to the caregiver. When fed and comfortable, the infant looks about herself, stares at a window or crib mobile, and reaches for it.

Therefore, prior to 5 months or so, while we assume an original and slowly unfolding sense of self and there is a substantial amount of activity that does not involve the caregiver, a major thrust of experiencing during periods of wakefulness seems to be in the context of the child's symbiotic relatedness to her mother.

We interrupt our detailing of the separation–individuation theory because a note regarding our use of the term *caregiver* is warranted. The caregiver we have in mind is the mother. We can also speak somewhat similarly of the father, occasionally of a sibling. We mean those caregivers who invest emotionally in the infant in that very unique, "family" way.

The caregiver who is a substitute for the mother or the father—say the caregiver who comes in when Mother goes to work away from home—may invest emotionally in and be valued by the infant. However, this caregiver does not bring to that investment of the child the quality of emotional experiencing typical for the parent. It is impossible for a caregiver who is not the parent to invest emotionally in the child at the same level and with the quality typical of parents.

In the course of our years of work with mothers, one mother made this point amply clear for us. As she talked about her neighbor's children, whom she found enormously attractive and toward whom she felt a great deal of affection, she tried to sort out the difference between how she felt about her own children and how she felt about these lovely neighbor children. She decided the major difference was that if she felt about her neighbor's children as she did about her own, she would not be able to tolerate the pain of leaving them in the evening.

However much a caregiver substituting for the parents attaches to her ward, however much a teacher invests emotionally in her students, however much a doctor invests emotionally in her patients—that degree of emotional investment cannot (and should not) reach the level, the depth, or the quality of attachment characteristic of that which parents invest in their children.

To highlight this critical difference in relatedness and attachments, mental health professionals sometimes speak of parents and children as primary objects (*object* meaning person), who form primary attachments to and relationships with one another, in contrast to the secondary attachments and relationships we form with people we value who might be our neighbors, our friends, our teachers, and so forth. The caregiver about whom we have been speaking so far refers to primary caregivers—the parents.

Now, let's resume our detailing of separation–individuation theory. At about 5 to 6 months of age, the child begins to experience a significant heightening of her awareness of herself and to gradually clarify the distinction between self and the caregiver. For example, 5½-month-old Susan, while sitting on Mother's lap, seemed to pull away from her mother's body, as if to look better at the bustle around her with new interest. She seemed to be awakened from her earlier state of comfortable encapsulation with Mother, molded into her on her lap. She seemed much more alert, "ready to go," so to speak, and older. Mahler spoke of this experiencing as *hatching*. Susan seemed as if she was pushing out of her symbiotic oneness with Mother.

As this often-seen example suggests, at the midpoint of the first year of life, a second maturational differentiation and heightening of both physiologic and psychological processes occurs. With it there is a major differentiation and heightening in aggression. This is a nondestructive trend in aggression, manifest by increasing assertiveness and increasing sensorimotor activity. We see increasing locomotion, an ability and interest in exploring, an increased capability in sensory modalities, and an increased capacity in cognitive functioning (as Piaget described). At this point, the infant thrusts into the process of separation–individuation. This occurs in two major subphases. The first subphase runs from about 5 to 6 months on through about 16 months of age. The second stage runs from 16 months of age to 3 years. (Dr. Mahler subdivided both into yet another subdivision, but this latter subdivision is not essential for this exposition.)

In the beginning, the first of these two major subphases is characterized by the infant's pulling away from the mother, just as $5^1/_2$-month-old Susan was doing. Next the infant begins to exercise her increasing motor skills and evidences an increasing need to explore the environment. This gives one the impression that the infant wants to learn and understand what the environment is all about and is attempting to gain mastery over it. At the same time, the infant is attempting to gain mastery over her own newly emerging capabilities and skills. A marked thrust toward autonomy, separateness, and individuation becomes evident. Often, at this time, a 12-month-old infant may be so active, so busy, so pressed to explore everything (including putting things in her mouth) that many a mother experiences the infant as "getting into everything and causing all kinds of trouble and aggravation."

At the height of the thrust toward autonomy, the second major subphase of separation–individuation is initiated by the infant's increasing recognition that the mother and she are truly separate individuals. Increasing cognitive (thinking) skills begin to make clear to the 16- to 18-month-old that her relationship to the caregiver is not secured by an enveloping emotional membrane or an emotional oneness. Rather, it consists of being tied emotionally to the caregiver, as two separate individuals. The tie, of course, is the profound emotional attachment that the child has already made to the mother and the mother has made to the child.

This heightened recognition of the self as separate from the mother initially brings with it an emotional crisis. This crisis is evidenced in behaviors that reveal anxiety and, at times, a benign form of depressive feelings that Drs. Mahler and McDevitt call "lowkeyedness." We also see behaviors that signal an internal struggle. Dr. Mahler emphasized that this internal struggle is produced by the infant's experiencing conflicting wishes. On the one hand, she wants to remain one with Mother, as if tied to Mother in a membrane. On the other hand, the infant experiences a powerful inner thrust to be an individual separate from that highly valued person, the mother. We can assume that a parallel, although somewhat different, process occurs within the relationship of the infant to the father, and perhaps even with siblings.

It might be useful to describe one common way the crisis Dr. Mahler and her colleagues talked about becomes evident in the behavior of many 16- to 24-month-old children. In some instances, this may occur earlier, and it may also occur somewhat later, which is not to be construed as either good or bad.

When Candy was 1 year, 7 months, and 21 days of age, we witnessed a sharply delineated crisis of the kind we are talking about. This particular morning, Candy stayed close to her mother from the beginning of our group session. Four other children, whom she knew well, took off their shoes and went to our playroom. Candy, who was close to her mother on "their" sofa busily playing with toys, saw what they were up to and took off her shoes, too, excitedly readying herself to join the others. However, once her shoes were off, her mood sobered and she climbed back onto the sofa with some help from her mother. Five seconds after she had climbed onto her mother's lap, Candy began to cry and twist her body away from mother, giving the impression that she was suddenly experiencing acute pain. Puzzled, her mother sensitively responded to her child's cues by putting Candy down. Candy dropped to the floor, crying, twisting, and kicking her legs in a mild tantrum — a reaction most unusual for her. Surprised, her mother tried to comfort Candy by talking and touching. Finally, through mutual accord, mother picked Candy up. But once in her mother's arms, Candy again started to cry and twist herself away. Again, her puzzled mother complied and put Candy down. Mother and daughter twice again enacted this same sequence. It wound down with the sixth hold-me-close communication. Candy's pain and distress — which we inferred arose from her conflicting wishes to be close to while at the same time be separate from her mother — were strikingly mirrored in the feelings of confusion her mother showed.[2]

This mother was at first bewildered by the child's behavior, and was much relieved when we explained what we believed was going on in her child. It made sense to her.

---

[2]H. Parens, *The Development of Aggression in Early Childhood* (New York: Jason Aronson, 1979), p. 227.

Two points are especially important for parents to be aware of, because each presents an opportunity to enhance the positive quality of the parent–child relationship and all that follows from it. The first is that the infant in the first subphase of the separation–individuation phase is powerfully thrust by an inner need to exercise self feelings and self-motivated activities. This remarkable thrust toward autonomy needs to be protected by the parent. This is done by facilitating the 1-year-old's opportunities for exploration, so that the exercise of emerging skills can be carried out under conditions that are safe and allow for excitement, learning, and mastery. The parent's awareness of the child's powerful thrust to autonomy and effectiveness will facilitate her reacting to her child's inner thrust in growth-prompting ways. (Chapters 4 and 5 are especially pertinent to this issue.)

The second point is that, during the second subphase of the separation–individuation process, the infant will at times experience the awareness of being truly separate from the mother as anxiety producing. This usually occurs under two conditions. The first is when the infant perceives the self as separate from the mother at a time when this perception leads to an acute feeling of helplessness and of not being ready for that separateness. This can bring with it anxiety and a depressive feeling that Mahler and McDevitt called "lowkeyedness." We assume this "lowkeyedness" is the product of an inner feeling of loss, of losing that all-encompassing relatedness with the primary caregiver. The second condition that may produce acute anxiety at this time occurs in the context of the experience of, on the one hand wanting to remain one with Mother, while on the other hand wanting to be separate from her. Mahler felt this creates an emotional crisis in the child, as we saw in Candy. It usually occurs between 18 and 24 months of age, although we always allow for schedule variation.

Both types of conditions, characteristic of the second part of the separation–individuation phase, will tend to lead to the reemergence of or heightening of separation anxiety and stranger responsiveness. We often find the resurgence of these reactions and the clinging they bring are sometimes alarming to mothers. Some mothers feel that the toddler, who two weeks ago freely moved away from her and was an explorer of her universe, has suddenly become an infant again, regressing, needing to cling, experiencing a heightened degree of separation and stranger anxieties. Many mothers construe this to be a loss of gains made earlier. In fact, this is an advance, signaling the infant's move from the first major subphase of separation-individuation into the second.

It is important for the parent to be aware of the fact that this second peak of separation anxiety and stranger anxiety is tied up with the potential stabilizing of a sense of self, of the tolerance of separateness from the caregiver. Both of these, we want to underscore, will be enhanced by the caregiver making herself available for holding, comforting, and reassuring as this process is worked through. In other words, it is important for parents to allow the child's clinging, to give comfort when the infant experiences anxiety. The toddler is now attempting to separate, individuate, and consolidate the experience of self as separate from the other. This is occurring in a relatedness that is strongly held together by an emotional attachment of a more mature order than that which occurred during the symbiotic phase.

What we have talked about so far pertains to the development of the relationship between child and parent during the first three years of life. The major thrust of that development occurs in the two-some relatedness (dyad) of infant and parent. All parents know that during these first three years of life, the infant is highly capable of experiencing resentment and anger toward the primary caregiver, as when the mother or father pays attention to another person. This kind of interaction is generally more complex than two-some interaction. We speak of it as a triadic, or three-some interaction.

The early forms of triadic relatedness bring with them conflicts which, of course, need to be dealt with by the parent in growth-promoting ways. Early experiences of rivalry and wanting the mother all to oneself need to be dealt with emphatically, with reassurance, with a clear recognition of the rights of all siblings to a relationship with the parent, with assurance that one sibling is not more important to the parent than the others. Ultimately, each child will experience this as highly reassuring and protective. Although each child would like to be the only child, the experience of being preferred over another child invariably brings the threat that someday, when she is bad, she will no longer be the preferred child and will be demoted to being the less-cared-for member of the family. Equality among siblings in the eyes of the parents is highly desirable and needs to be protected.

Psychoanalytic clinicians and child developmentalists

have long established that at about two and a half years of age, a development of enormous consequence to the child emerges. This dramatically changes and shapes the relationship between child and parents. It is the emergence of infantile sexuality and with it, the Oedipus complex.

The Emergence of Infantile Sexuality and Its Impact on Relatedness

Parents who are able to let themselves see them will note the following types of behaviors in their children that pertain to their emerging sexuality. Although infants younger than 2 years of age pay attention to and touch their own genitals from time to time, at about $2^1/_2$ years, the increased frequency and persistence with which they do so is often quite striking. Parents will, in other words, note an increase in "infantile masturbation." They will also notice a new or increased interest in, and tender attention to, babies, especially so in little girls. The child will also begin to ask many questions about babies. Again, this is especially so in little girls. The child will begin to ask all kinds of questions about genitals—her own and those of others, especially her siblings and parents. Parents will note that when children $2^1/_2$, 3, and 4 play games, they often play "house."

Another more complex type of behavior can be also observed: Quite often, a girl's relationship with her mother becomes more openly conflicted and troublesome. One experienced mother, who up to now had a very warm relationship with her 27-month-old daughter, found things were becoming quite difficult between them. One day, when her daugher was 30 months old, the mother jokingly asked, "Anyone want her for a year?" Another little girl, just under 3 years of age, who also had a good relationship with her mother, dumped her mother's perfumes and powders in the toilet on several occasions. One time she did so after she had put some on herself.

The first little girl told her mother that she would like to go on a trip alone with her father. The second little girl, according to the father's report, fluttered her eyelashes at him and asked him to take her dancing and to the movies. A similar, parallel phenomenon occurs in the little boy with relation to his mother and father. That is to say, a 3-year-old complained to his mother that he did not want his father to come home for dinner that night.

What causes these behaviors? Psychoanalysts have long proposed that they are propelled by psychobiological maturation in the sexual drive. This drive, a powerful force in the service of the preservation of the species, makes its first true appearance about the third year of life and leads to the above behaviors, which are identified as part of infantile sexuality. These dramatic developments in a child's relationship to her mother and father have been conceptualized as the Oedipus complex.

The Oedipus complex unfolds like this. At about 2 years of age, a parent first notes her child's increased interest in her own genitals. This includes their manipulation through the child's using her hand or some other indirect means. With it, a parent also begins to hear questions about genitals: "Does so and so have a penis?" or "Where is so and so's penis?" One little girl insistently demanded that her mother show her her penis! The first genital feelings seem to not be directed toward anyone in particular—it could be Mother's or Father's knee—or they are sometimes directed toward hard objects, such as toys. These first feelings do not seem to be directed preferentially toward one parent or the other.

Then, at about 2½ years of age, the child's sexual feelings tend to become more selective. In little boys, they tend to be preferentially directed toward their mothers. In little girls, dominantly but not exclusively, they tend to be directed toward their fathers. Although the prior attachments to both Mother and Father significantly remain the same, some degree of modification now begins to occur. As we mentioned before, one little girl who had a very warm relationship with her mother prior to 2 years of age now began to experience a good deal of difficulty in it.

A question one might ask at this time is: If all of this is so, why does the child turn his or her sexual feelings toward his or her own mother or father? Isn't that a bit unwise on the part of nature? Why not to just any male or female? Would it not be even better if these feelings, from the outset, were attached to someone other than one's parents, to protect against incest?

Generally, at this time in development, the child seems to be quite determinedly selective: For the boy, it tends to be his mother; for the girl, her father. We assume that this happens for the following reason. The sensual feelings the child is newly experiencing tend to follow the path forged by the affectionate feelings she has. By this age, these are already well stabilized in the child's relationships to her parents. This—along with the seemingly inherent tendency of sexual feelings to be heterosexual—is why the little girl selectively turns to her father with her sexual feelings, rather than to the postman, and the little boy turns to his mother rather than his pretty neighbor. However, because the sexual drive is so powerful, even at this age, there is some spillover onto other persons.

It is when the sensual feelings become specifically directed toward the parent of the other sex that we find a little girl fluttering her eyelashes at her father and asking him to take her dancing and to the movies. Or she might say that she would like to go on a trip alone with her father. The little boy would like Father not to come home for dinner so he could be alone at home with his mother.

Of course, wishes such as these are reasonably frustrated. In fact, it is helpful that they be frustrated. It does not take much for the child to recognize that the gratification she yearns for and does not get from her father, someone else does get. Although Father does not take his lovely daughter dancing and to the movies, he does take her mother. And the little boy, of course, sees the same, as well.

As a result, intense feelings of jealousy erupt. The first little girl pretended that she was shooting her mother dead. The little boy wished that his father would not come home for dinner. This creates a significant conflict within the child: The little girl wants to shoot the mother she loves; the little boy wishes that the father he loves would not come home. We all know how feelings of jealousy bring enormous pain. This, of course, generates hostility and hate toward the loved parent of the same sex. It creates a substantially difficult and threatening conflict within the child, a conflict due to the child's feelings of ambivalence. Since the rival is one of the prime persons the child loves, and since the feelings of hostility and hate tend to be quite intense, the child feels a great deal of anxiety. Also, these circumstances arouse the threat of punishment of largest consequence. All in all, this creates an internal state—as well as an external situation—that demands the child's attention and large coping efforts.

The child cannot tolerate this conflict. In order to cope with it, she tends to do several things. First of all, she begins to feel acute guilt. This is the product of her developing a conscience that arises out of the conflict produced by the little girl hating and wanting to destroy her beloved mother. And similarly this occurs in the little boy for hating and wanting to destroy his beloved father.

Another thing that soon follows, although it does not occur right away, is that the little boy comes to terms with his conflicted wishes by trying to give up the wish to marry his mommy, and the little girl gives up her wish to marry her daddy.

What also follows from this conflict, is that the child attempts to tame and control the hostile feelings that have been generated within her toward the loved parent. Thereby she develops a greater capability to cope constructively with and master feelings of hostility generated within her, not only by this conflict, but also by other life events.

Still another thing follows: The child intensifies her identifications with—wants to be like—the parent of the same sex. A number of other highly salutary developments follow, as well. These include a heightening of the need to sublimate some wishes and feelings.

One more highly important event emerges from this conflict: The wishes that cannot be given up—the feelings of hate and rivalry that cannot be resolved by the young child by the time she is 5 or so years of age—become repressed. They are pushed into the child's unconscious part of the mind where, because they are not changed or resolved, they remain active.

Interestingly, the Oedipus complex also occurs in families where there is no father at home, for whatever reason. Just how a child reared in a one-parent family goes through this process is not firmly established. A number of factors probably play a part. Where there is no Father at home due to a separation or divorce, the child will often feel responsible for that separation because of her oedipal wishes. Or, quite often, the child "discovers" that Mother does have a man in her life. The child also knows that her father was there at one time, however briefly, and experiences her sexual wishes as transgressive. Also, a major contributor to the child's experiencing prohibitions against the gratification of sexual wishes comes from the parents, reactions to their expression. Responsible parents do, of course, prohibit sexual activity with them and tend to reject their children's amorous declarations of intent.

There are still unanswered questions on this matter. We

must also add the likelihood that 3- and 4-year-old children's cognitive capacities may contribute to the emergence of this complex. These include their abilities to take in what they see and hear, to think at a surprisingly sophisticated level, and to fantasize richly. Their inner sense or "knowledge"—possibly brought about by the stirrings in their young bodies—that reproduction requires male and female collaboration may contribute to the emergence of this complex, as well.

All in all, the unfolding of the Oedipus complex modifies dramatically the child's relationships to her mother and father and creates a large, internal emotional conflict. But, at the same time, it brings with it enormously salutary emotional and personality developments within the child.

Later Major Trends in Relationships

Let us say just a word about major trends in relationships that occur during the child's elementary-school years and adolescence.

Current social trends bring with them large modifications in psychic life, such as sending children to school earlier and placing them in day-care centers from the first months of life. Such trends unavoidably influence the character and the quality of relationships, sometimes for the better and sometimes not. Clearly, individual variations will be found.

Nonetheless, speaking in global terms, relationships change significantly during the elementary-school years.

As we have detailed above, the prime tasks of emotional development during the first 5 to 6 years of life center around the nuclear family. First, during the first 3 years, is the establishment of the self in relatedness with the parents—as, for instance, spelled out by separation-individuation theory. And second, from about $2^1/_2$ to 6 years of age, is the emergence and partial resolution of the Oedipus complex. Hand in hand with other factors, the resolution of the Oedipus complex pushes the child into relationships outside the nuclear family.

As we have said before, it is helpful to think of gradations of relationships, where those with parents and siblings are considered primary relationships and relationships with other adults and peers may be considered secondary relationships. This grading of relationships is dependent on the degree and quality of emotional attachment between a child and the other person. Bearing in mind this difference in both the character and the quality of relatedness, consider the following. The extent to which peers and other adults become important to a child less than 5 years of age depends on the quality of relationships with primary persons and the degree to which the child's needs are met, as well as the quality of relationships outside the home, with persons with whom the child forms secondary relationships. Children, of course, vary in their experiences in both sectors of relatedness, inside the home and outside the home. We are using a model that is simpler than actual life when we assert that primary relationships and the prime tasks of development during the first 5 years of life reside in and most optimally are dealt with within the nuclear family. But we do so because we believe it to be basically accurate. Within the framework of this model, secondary relationships can be strongly enriching, and may in fact play a vital salutary part, especially where primary relationships are impoverished.

Now let's get back to the point we want to make. No doubt the above-mentioned social trends impact on the character and quality of children's relationships. Nonetheless, the experience and partial resolution of the Oedipus complex pushes the 5- to 6-year-old child into relationships outside the nuclear family. At the same time, the child retains a deep emotional tie to her parents. During the elementary-school years, persons outside the home, both adults (teachers especially) and peers, become more and more important to the child. During this period especially, siblings, with whom children have primary relationships, are the great bridging relationships between the family and the outside world.

Peer relationships and relationships with teachers bring both gratifications and frustrations. Playing with one's friends is not always fun. Parents at times make the mistake of thinking that the child who was outside playing with her friends was having a great time.. When the child comes home, it is now time to set the table or do homework. The idea is: "You were out having fun; it is now time to get down to work!" The problem is, being out playing with friends may be painfully frustrating, disappointing, indeed, at times infuriating. Not uncommonly, one's friends want to do what they want to do, not what your child wants to do.

They may, in fact, abuse your child in the course of their own efforts to master their difficulties and the injuries to which they may be subjected.

The shift to persons outside the home is, however, highly limited during the elementary-school years. During these years, peers cannot yet serve the protective and caring functions parents serve; therefore they cannot be leaned on fully. In fact, parents continue to be vitally central in the child's life and are turned to for continuing development and mastery of life's increasingly larger demands.

The next phase of development brings with it a dramatic shift in relationships. Adolescence brings remarkable changes that we all know. These include: bodily changes that transform the child into the adult-to-be; the challenging and exciting upsurge of sexuality and aggression; the further evolving of the self and ongoing consolidation of one's identity; large strides in cognitive (mental) skills and intellectual development; the mood swings these changes and challenges bring with them.

Crucial among these changes is a major shift in relationships, from the parents' being the central persons of the younger child's life to gradually making peers the central persons in relationships. This shift in relationships, which takes about a decade in its course, is a task that should be well underway by the age of twenty. The shift from having parents at the center of the person's life to having a peer at the center is concluded during young adulthood. The parents' ability to allow and, where needed, guide and support the teenager's efforts to make this important shift in relationships is important during adolescence. As we all know, this progression in relationships is a complex one, replete with difficulties and anxieties.

One of the major difficulties for parents is that the adolescent traverses this stage with a good deal of difficulty. This is particularly evidenced in mood swings, in the need to be very close to the parents at one time and to want nothing to do with them at another; to be proud of the parents at one time and be highly embarrassed by them at another. All of this leads, at times, to highly conflicted relatedness between the adolescent and her parents. There are also difficulties in being close to parents that are associated with the realistic need for separateness and individuality, the need to depreciate the parents, the need to reject the parents' beliefs and attitudes, and more. Relationships between parents and adolescents vary widely. Much depends on the quality of these relationships as they evolve in the course of development, as well as on the experiences the adolescent has outside the home.

Further Thoughts on Optimizing the Parent–Child Relationship

Hand in hand with understanding one's children, we believe it is critical that parents trust their own perceptions and feelings as a guide to effectively dealing with their children's aggression.

It is well established in the mental health field that in

order to develop optimally, we all need to be involved in human relationships that are characterized by a positive emotional investment, by open, direct, and honest communication about emotional experiences, and by a sufficient degree of responsiveness to our needs for emotional involvement as well as for individuality or autonomy. When parents are able to form such relationships with their children, development is most likely to proceed as optimally as the child's inborn givens will allow. Then the child develops the capacity to be positively involved with others alongside the capacity to function at an age-appropriate independent level, and the development of excessive hostility is minimized.

We have to underscore the fact that even when personality development proceeds optimally, it is still quite difficult. For one thing, development and change bring not only the excitement and pleasure of being able to do new things, but also anxiety over what is new, strange, and uncertain. Among the many difficulties that normally occur, development brings sadness over inevitable losses brought about by growing up, anger over hurts, and sometimes guilt over becoming more and more self-reliant and separate from those we love. In other words, strong and disturbing feelings such as anger, anxiety, sadness, and guilt result not only when there are external problems or interferences. They also occur when development is proceeding well. However, when development is proceeding optimally, there are large stretches of time when the predominant feeling a child or an adolescent has is one of delight and joy, accompanied by interest, curiosity, and energy for independent initiative, exploration, and work, as well as for investment in important relationships.

Development does not occur in a straight line. It has many ups and downs. Also, development usually proceeds in small steps. The developmental progress may go unnoticed except at milestones like the baby's first smiles, steps, words, kindergarten, first grade, or high-school graduation. Adding to the stresses that development brings, we find that the inner pressure to develop and to master is such that once we achieve mastery and competence in one area, we seldom pause to savor our accomplishments. We almost immediately begin working on another new developmental task or return to an old, recurrent, still insufficiently mastered one.

Growth is accompanied by regression, and even by temporary disorganization. This is so when basic aspects of a child's organization are changing and developing positively but have not yet stabilized. At these crossroads of development, we may see regression or disorganization against a background of small, but significant, signs of growth and a basically positive mood. For example: A child who is beginning to see herself more as a separate individual, and feels strong and delighted by it, may temporarily evidence brief periods of distress and cling to Mother. The parent's being available to deal with the distress and, at the same time to acknowledge the child's developing sense of individuality, helps to stabilize the child's new capabilities. The child will sense not only the parent's emotional avail-

The child will sense not only the parent's emotional availability, but also the parent's recognition and approval of
her growth and the parent's confidence and reliability in
times of uncertainty. More than likely, she will begin to
internalize her parent's helpful response to growth and
change.

It helps if one is able to have a positive attitude about the
inevitable ups and downs that occur during the course of
the child's development. It helps to recognize that when old
troubles reappear, difficult as it may be, this is another
opportunity for the child and parent to master them. There
are many instances when caring for a child and responding
to her needs provide a major developmental challenge and
opportunity for mastery and growth—for both child and
parents.

In helping our children develop as individuals who can
form good relationships, it is crucial we understand emotional communication and be open to it. One of the basic
ways communicating occurs is by the child's interacting
with her parent in such a way that the parent comes to have
a similar or a complementary emotional experience to that
of the child. The child induces an emotional response in
her parents. Part of Candy's mother's bewilderment (above
in this chapter) arose from her empathically experiencing
her child's bewilderment.

For the most part, this communication by means of
empathy happens automatically, outside both the child's
and parent's awareness. By being emotionally available and
attentive, the parent may find herself having very powerful

child, and yet she may not be able to understand these or respond helpfully. This is especially so with intense emotions such as rage, hate, guilt, anxiety, and sadness, which can, of course, be most unpleasant. In addition, no parent likes to feel rage toward or anxiety about her child. Together, these can lead a parent to ignore or be overwhelmed and immobilized by her emotional experience.

When this occurs, the parent is less likely to be effective in helping the child than at other times. This is true not only because the parent's feeling overwhelmed may be immobilizing or compel the parent to ignore the child's communication, but also because the parent's emotional experiencing is crucial to her understanding the child's experiencing. The parent's emotional experiencing represents a basic point of contact with the child. It is her most important source of information about the child's inner experience at that moment, and the best guide to a helpful intervention.

However, we must add a note of caution here: A parent should not always assume that she and the child are feeling the same emotions. To do so may simply be inaccurate, and it risks interfering with the child's sense of separateness and individuality. It is important for parents to try to understand their own anger and rage and to express them reasonably, rather than with hostility. If in doing so, the feeling is either too intense or in some way not characteristic of the parent's usual mode of experiencing, the parent should consider that her child may be inducing such a feeling in her. A quick review of the recent interaction could well help to decide whether or not this is a likely possibility. If so, then the parent can use this understanding in coming up with a helpful intervention. If the parent's understanding is accurate and the intervention appropriate, the parent will often see a positive effect on the child's feelings and behavior, although that may not happen immediately.

Here is a brief example to illustrate this empathic process in which a child induces rage in a parent who, through some quick thinking, uses her experiencing to come up with a helpful intervention, rather than becoming overly hostile toward her child.

> A mother of a 2-year-old boy found it necessary to set firm limits to protect her child when he tried to experiment with his finger in a light socket. However, because she was in a rush, she had been more brusque than usual in her limit setting, and had neglected to explain the reasons for these limits or deal with the child's angry response to her limit setting. She quickly found herself engaged in a series of unpleasant interactions with her child, in which she began to feel pushed around, controlled, and full of rage, with the impulse to yell and strike out at her child.
>
> At this point, she stopped herself and began to try to understand her feelings. She was startled by the intensity of her anger – indeed, rage – and asked herself if she could be feeling what her child was feeling. Reviewing their recent interactions, she realized that her setting limits, even though necessary, had led him to be angry. But her not explaining the reasons for her limits and not taking the time to deal with his anger may have led him to experience her limits as pushing him around and overcontrolling him, which brought him feelings of rage.
>
> She could then explain to her child the reasons for the

limits, apologize for not having done so sooner, and explain why she had neglected to do so. Then, calmer herself, she found that her son was ready to be comforted by her. By working to understand her rage, she was able to interrupt an escalating hostile interaction and help her child deal with his own anger.

Finally, let's consider two other instances in which a child may induce feelings of anger in an emotionally available parent. First—an instance quite difficult to read and often not thought of—is when a child deliberately opposes a parent in order to separate psychologically from the parent and assert her autonomy. Here the child uses anger to create emotional distance in order to further the process of becoming a self, a separate and individual person. This is especially palpable when a 2-year-old, for instance, responds to his mother's offer of a food he likes, say ice cream, with a reflexive "No!" It may be the same when a young child (some adolescents will do this type of thing, as well) touches Mother's hot cup of coffee in the face of her prohibition and will not stop until her limit setting becomes a warning of punishment. It is important that the parent acknowledge the child's need for autonomy, and at the same time be positively available when the child is ready to restore closeness in the relationship he has temporarily needed to disrupt.

Next, a child may provoke anger in a parent in order to see how the parent deals with such a distressing feeling—one that the child herself finds so difficult to experience and deal with. Again, this is usually done outside of awareness.

deal with. Again, this is usually done outside of awareness. The child is testing: Can mother feel angry without being overwhelmed, without having a tantrum, without becoming destructive, without having to ignore the feeling? If the parent can do so, then the child gains useful experience in managing anger and is likely to internalize this event, identify with her parent, and learn to manage her own anger better.

In both examples, it is helpful if the child can see that the parent's anger is outweighed by the parent's love for the child. This happens if the parent, though angry, does not become overly hostile and/or stay angry too long. This indicates to the child that the parent can be angry at the child and still love her at the same time.

The Quality of Relatedness Largely Determines the Quality of the Child's Aggression

In discussing how to help our children cope with their aggression, we have emphasized the central importance of a positive emotional attachment between child and parents for enhancing healthy aggressiveness (e.g., assertiveness) and for preventing the development of excessive hostility. Love, evidence of affection toward our children, respect for them and their sensitivities, empathy and efforts to understand their behaviors and communications from the time they are born—all contribute centrally to the evolving of a positive attachment. Where such experiencing was not possible "from birth on," it is never too late to start interacting with our children or adolescents this way.

We have emphasized that a positive attachment is the largest insurance parents have toward helping their children cope better with the anger, hostility, and hate that normal development brings with it. We must again underline that even the best of child rearing brings with it many experiences of excessive unpleasure and, therewith, of hostility and hate toward one's own parents. Limit setting, which is needed in every child's rearing, is a prime producer of excessive unpleasure. So are unavoidable separations, such as a mother's need to go to work outside the home every morning. Parents' emotional states may lead them to be temporarily unavailable, thereby causing excessive unpleasure in their children. However, this may be dealt with in a growth-promoting manner.

> For example, a father who was grieving the loss of his own father was too turned inward to respond to his 4-year-old son, Tommy, who just fell and hurt his knee. Tommy, seeing his father withdrawn, sulks, but says nothing. One-half hour later, as if coming out of a cloud, Father awakens to what had happened. He takes occasion then, when he and Tommy are together, to tell him, "You know, I saw that you fell. I'm sorry. I was thinking about Grandpa and feeling very sad. Are you okay?" Tommy points to his knee without saying a word. Father says: "Let me see it." Tommy seems to resist for an instant, but he comes to his father, pats him on the shoulder, and says, "It's okay, Daddy." Indeed, he comforted his father.

In instances such as these, acknowledging a lapse of emotional availability can be reparative in and of itself.

The better secured the positive attachment between child and parent, the better the child will be able to deal constructively with the hostility mobilized within her. This will lead not only to the resolution of that hostility and hate, but also to healthier adaptation and the capacity for learning and sublimations. Positive attachment favors less intense ambivalence and its better resolution over time.

Love is unquestionably the most critical ingredient needed for rearing our children well. Of course, we cannot teach parents to love. Fortunately, most parents experience profound love feelings toward their children. However, even though critical and essential, love is not enough to secure growth-promoting child rearing. Let us add a few other cardinal factors that are specifically related to the importance of loving our children in helping them deal with their aggression. Parents can enhance the positive valence of attachment, which is so crucial to protecting against the development of excessive hostility, in the following manner.

Parents need to be *sufficiently emotionally available* to their child from infancy through adolescence. To be emotionally available means that one is not only sufficiently present physically, but that one is available for emotional interaction when it is needed.

There are going to be times when parents will not be able to be physically or emotionally available to their children. When you cannot be emotionally available to your child, that emotional availability ought to be made possible soon thereafter. One can make up for not being emotionally available at a given time of need by being so at a time soon thereafter. If a parent is busy at work and cannot be disturbed by a telephone call from an anxious child, it can be made clear that the parent will call as soon as possible.

One does not have to always be responsive to a child at the moment of need, if the child has learned the parent will be responsive as soon as possible. Of course, "as soon as possible" has its limits. As soon as possible cannot be two years from now; nor can a parent promise himself to be responsive to his child when the child is an adolescent. We are speaking of the need to be responsive at intervals of time such as one, two, or perhaps even five hours.

Of course, there are conditions when a young child will be able to wait for longer than that. For instance, if Mother is sick and unavailable for several days, the young child will be able to integrate the fact that the mother is sick and cannot be responsive to the child's needs until she feels better. But if the young child can see that there is nothing particularly wrong with the parent, and if the parent cannot make herself available to the child for periods that go beyond hours or several days, the child is likely to feel the parent is not sufficiently emotionally available.

Another cardinal ingredient needed by every parent is the capacity to be *empathic*. It is important for parents to try to feel, to perceive, and then to understand what the child is experiencing and what the child's behavior is about. This is so whether the child is very young or an adolescent. Since empathy is the ability to feel what another person may feel, without actually experiencing it to the same degree oneself, the best way to enhance one's capacity for empathy is to put oneself in the child's shoes and try to feel what that is like.

Then react to the child from the vantage point of this experiencing. After all, we all know this phenomenon well from the old adage, "Do unto others as you would have others do unto you." In rearing children, this principle can have remarkable benefits to both child and parent.

The parent who is empathic and respects her young child will be able to nurture when it is needed and will be able to better determine whether that child needs to be held or allowed off the lap. The parent's empathy will help in determining when the child needs to do things herself, needs to exercise her strivings for autonomy and self-development.

We often hear mothers tell us that they have been told that if they "hold their infants too much," it will make the infant become too dependent. That, in general, is an error. Although it is true that parents may hold their infants too much, this usually occurs when a parent is not reading the infant's expressed wishes and needs well. For instance, a mother who insists that her infant stay on her lap, when the infant is giving clear evidence of wanting to slide off her lap, is imposing her wish for closeness without being aware of the infant's wish for separateness. However, the child's expressed wishes are discernable from neonatal life on. The parent's empathic reading and sensitivity to these communications will help the parent be appropriately responsive to the child's needs, whether they are to be picked up and held or to be let down. Gestural language is most often very clear, even well before the child can speak. For instance, we all know that the need for closeness is usually expressed in young children by the outstretching of arms toward the parent, by clinging to the mother's leg, by pulling toward and/or onto the mother. On the other hand, the child's wish to move away from the mother is usually expressed by turning away from the mother, squirming to get off the mother's lap, or pulling away from the mother. Of course, the mother's appropriate responsiveness to these behaviors will secure that she is providing the gratification that is commensurate with the child's need. This will mean that the balance of the child's needs to be close or separate will be respected.

Therefore, it is inaccurate to say that the mother's holding her young child in response to her child's expressed need to be held will lead the infant to become too dependent. In fact, when young children are held when they ask for it, they are less likely to continue to feel the need to be held. Therefore they are less likely to become overly dependent and clinging than will be the case when their need to be held is too often frustrated. Such frustrated needs continue to clamor for gratification and foster a greater degree of neediness. Furthermore, every mother knows that toddlers do not tend to stay on their mother's laps too long when they feel secure.

Intimately tied up with the need for empathy is the need for *respecting the child.* By respecting the child, we have in mind maintaining a continual awareness, even from birth, that the child is a person, with sensitivities and vulnerabilities as well as strengths and capabilities—all commensurate with her age. What indicates respect for the child can be better determined when the parent asks herself, "Would I want to be treated the way I am treating my child?"

Respecting the child should begin from the child's birth on, in fact, while the child is still in the mother's uterus! It will enhance the capacity for empathy. It will make the parent more aware of the child's—be she an infant or adolescent—needs for closeness, for comforting, for instruction; as well as her needs for separateness, for experiencing the self and parent as two persons and the self as an individual that is separate from those the child loves.

By *engaging in activities* with her young child that are growth promoting, a parent enhances: the development of trust; the development of a sense of self; the development of a sense that one can do things oneself; the development of skills, of rules, and the capacity to learn. This can be done by playing age-appropriate games and by responding to experiences with an effort to teach the child—as parents automatically do, for instance, in teaching their children words, how to count, and in helping them learn how to walk.

When parents engage in activities—especially in play—with their children, be it an infant or a teenager, a great deal occurs that can marvelously enhance the quality of the parent–child relationship. When you can find occasions to teach your children about things—such as how and why a cup of juice spills, or how grabbing the paper cup too hard makes it collapse and spill its contents—not only are you teaching your child her first lessons in physics, you are doing more than just facilitating the process of learning. When parents play with their children, they usually do so under conditions in which both child and parent are potentially, if not actually, enjoying each other's company and are in a good mood. When parents play with their children, the interaction tends to be highly favorable for optimizing the parent–child relationship, even when inter-action may at moments become troublesome, as in compet-itive games.

However, a problem may occur when parents fail to empathize with the child's experiencing and carry the play too far. For instance, not uncommonly Father may go too far in roughhousing with his toddler. He may go beyond the toddler's tolerance for heightened activity. This then leads the toddler to experience the roughhousing as dis-turbing. We have all heard a mother, annoyed with Father, tell him that he is always too rough with the child! How-ever, roughhousing, where a father can keep an eye on the child's tolerance for that play, can bring with it great pleasure, excitement, gratification, and feelings of affection. Empathic fathers can be a lot of fun!

Of course, in playing with the older child, there is also the problem of how to handle rules and how to handle losing. Dealing with these issues requires a great deal of sensitivity and skill on the part of parents. All in all, however, play between children and parents tends to be a period of warm, loving, mutually affectionate interaction, even where there are disappointments, and tends to be retained in memory. These memories can then counter those times when parents and children are at odds with each other and hostility is being generated in the child.

We want to emphasize the importance of *talking to your children* from the beginning of life. It is highly worthwhile to explain things to one's children. What made something happen, what made the parent angry with the child, when the parent will have to go out, when the parent will come back, and much more, need to be explained. Talking, giving explanations, and answering children's questions all contribute to enhancing the positive quality of the parent–child relationship. This does not mean that parents may not, at times, claim the need for rest or to do other work and not be able to talk to the child. But it is important to be aware of the merits of talking to your child. We have long emphasized to parents that if they want their adolescents to talk to them in times of stress and need, they should begin that process by talking to their children from the time they are babies.

Last but not least, *respect yourself*. Make a commitment to help your child develop as well as possible. Work to form a positive relationship with your child. Work to help your child cope with her own aggression. No one will try as much or as hard as you, and no one will have as valuable and effective an impact. Listen to your child and try to be as honest as possible. Try to understand what is happening between you and your child, and what your child needs.

Then, don't be too hard on yourself or expect too much of yourself. Parenting is hard work. Parents sometimes feel angry and guilty, too. Development is not a straight line for a child, and neither is it for a parent. Parents, too, experience periods of disorganization and regression as they grow in their parenting. This is a part of development. Learn from the rough times and from those unavoidable times when you don't do as well as you would like as a parent. The important thing is to keep trying to help your child.

Your child will recognize and appreciate your genuine efforts, even if what you do is not the most helpful at that moment. You will have plenty of opportunity for repair. Trust your own feelings and perceptions. Above all, notice and enjoy what you and your child are doing right.

CHAPTER 10

Recapitulation

In Chapter 1 we presented a model for understanding what aggression is, what it does to children, and what arouses it in them. We did this in the hope of helping parents find ways to promote what is healthy in aggression and prevent or mitigate the problems aggression causes children, parents, and society.

We have proposed that aggression develops: The elements of aggression we are born with and the tendencies for its activation are shaped by the experiences we have.

The part aggression plays in our lives is large. Much of it is visible to all of us. Along with sexuality and the development of self, aggression is one the great motivators of behavior and a great producer of internal mental conflicts. Parents have the great opportunity, and the heavy responsibility, of helping their children enhance its adaptive and creative potentials and cope with its destructive potentials.

Helping our children adapt optimally to the aggression within them can best occur in the arena of its activation in the relationships with their parents. No one will have as large an influence on how children's aggression develops than the child himself and his parents. The play of aggression toward self and others—where it is ultimately of most consequence—emerges within and gets its basic patterns of activation, modulation, and discharge within the parent–child relationship. This is its workshop.

In the course of years of observation and work with children and their parents (mothers mostly), we came to see that events occur between parent and child where aggression is strongly at play. In these interactions, depending on the parent's handling, aggression in the child can be enhanced toward its healthier development or pushed toward unhealthy development. We know from our work that much can be done to promote the healthier development of aggression, which is a force so vitally needed for healthy adaptation and successful living, and yet is so readily capable of causing pain and serious problems.

It has not been our intention to touch on all aspects of aggression; that is not necessary. As we said earlier, when parents understand key emotional experiences that meaningfully affect their children and are challenging to their parenting, what they learn in dealing with one experience can be applied with ingenuity to others. We have also found that parents take what they learn with us about their infants and apply it to their teenagers, also with marvelous ingenuity. They found that the principles—as spelled out in the chapters above—apply to rearing children at any age. With this in mind, we decided that if we could help parents have a clearer view of what happens in a limited number of typical and frequently occurring interactions between them

and their children, this could serve them in all its occur-
rences, because of the parents' marvelous commitments to
their children, their ingenuity, and their constant efforts to
solve problems and cope.

In fact, we found that certain critical events occur frequently, in which parents stand at the crossroads of
healthy and troublesome development. Parents all know
this and are most concerned about it. One road may lead to
harm, another to growth and mental health.

Children are not fragile, although they are sensitive.
What parents do matters greatly. Fortunately, we do get
many chances in our parenting. This is because development occurs over many years and mistakes can be repaired—all kinds of mistakes. As long as the mistakes were
not too harsh or repeated too often, and occurred at the
hands of parents who love their children, respect them, and
mean well, they are rectifiable. We found that we could
cluster many parent–child interactions, so we selected six
points of interaction between child and parent where
assertiveness can be enhanced and undue hostility mitigated. We found such critical events were notably clear and
definable. Once recognized, we found that such events can
readily be influenced for the good of both child and parent.

1. *Dealing constructively with experiences of excessive
unpleasure*, we have emphasized, is dealing at the threshold
of the mobilization of hostility. We all need to be able to be
angry and, at times, appropriately hostile. But we must
recognize and deal with it constructively, because excessive
hostility creates all sorts of problems for the self and for
others. The best place to govern whether our children's

hostility will become excessive or not is at the threshold of its generation (production).

2. *Allowing sufficient and reasonable autonomy* in large part means baby proofing the house, as Dr. Spock said many years ago. This has long been known to prevent hazardous situations for the young child. But it also is a means of preventing excessive frustration and decreases the chance of hostility being generated. Baby proofing the house also decrease the frequency of battles of wills between parent and young child, which will further decrease the generation and mobilization of hostility and ambivalence.

Furthermore, baby proofing also protects the child's energetic thrust toward autonomy, assertiveness, and mastery, and promotes interest and learning. All parents know that learning begins well before their child goes to school. Eight-month-old infants begin to display a high degree of curiosity and interest, which are inherent in their exploratory activity. We find them to be beginning explorers of their universe, in pursuit of their interest with great energy and pleasure. This pleasure, though, can easily be thwarted—indeed, changed to unpleasure—when the child's explorations are too often frustrated. This is where being a student begins, and we are convinced that if this early interest and pleasure in learning is protected and harnessed by the parents, their children will be encouraged to be students. Making the home safely explorable can contribute to this in important ways.

3. *Setting limits* is one of the most problematic encounters between child and parent. Prohibiting a child's action in his best interest begins earlier than we like, takes more

out of us than we expect, and creates problems by mobilizing hostility in both child and parent. Setting limits unavoidably produces ambivalence in both child and parent. This ambivalence significantly contributes to difficulties in human relationships, as well as in oneself. We find limit setting to be a critical event, and universally difficult. Here, too, the parent can choose many ways; some will be highly constructive, others will not. Understanding that the limit setting needed to rear children well unavoidably makes all parents angry with the children they love may lessen the guilt many parents feel at that juncture of rearing their children.

4. *Teaching the child how to cope with and express anger and hostility in reasonable and acceptable ways* is at the heart of the matter. Understanding what aggression is, that there is aggression that is needed for adaptation, work, and leading a productive life, as well as aggression that can harm and destroy self and others, helps parents determine what is acceptable and unacceptable in anger and hostility. Knowing that excessive unpleasure is what mobilizes hostility in children will make many parents realize their children are not "evil" when they are angry, but rather that they are experiencing excessive distress. This is what makes them hostile. Also, knowing that parents must at times frustrate and "step on their children's toes," can help them understand why the children they love sometimes hate them. Helping children reasonably express such burdensome feelings protects them enormously.

5. *Dealing with rage reactions and tantrums* are among the most challenging and critical events in development—for

both child and parent. Probably more than any other parent–child interaction, tantrums produce problems for parents and problems with the development of aggression in the child. Not only are tantrums bewildering expressions of excessive hostility, but because they cause excessive pain, tantrums can generate more hostility and rage in the child. Rather than just being discharges of high levels of hostility and hate, rage reactions and tantrums perpetuate these feelings. We have talked about the noxious influence of tantrums on development: Tantrums disorganize, over-whelm, make the child (and often the parent) feel helpless and in despair. We urge parents not to be intimidated by them. Make them a priority experience when they occur, setting other things aside to deal with them. Dealing con-structively with tantrums should be a priority for all of us.

6. Like all other sources of excessive unpleasure, *painful emotional feelings can mobilize hostility.* Although there are exceptions to this, for the most part, marked anxiety and depression will mobilize hostility, whether or not hostility is visible or directly expressed. Other feelings can produce much pain and have similar effects. For instance, shame can lead people to rage and the wish to undermine them-selves and others. Guilt can lead to an unrelenting need for harsh (self) punishment. Jealousy can lead to wishes for revenge. Although parents may not be able to make such feelings go away, they can help children cope with them and reduce their intensities.

7. And last, we have talked about dealing with aggres-sion constructively by optimizing the vehicle that guides the child through his long development: the relationship with his parents. *Optimizing the parent–child relationship* is,

we believe, the largest avenue toward promoting the healthy emotional development of our children. It brings with it, furthermore, greater gratification in our parenting and can significantly enrich our individual lives.

Index